THE CONSTITUTIONAL SYSTEM

The Group Character of the Elected Institutions

Henry J. Merry

New York
Westport, Connecticut
London

Library of Congress Cataloging-in-Publication Data

Merry, Henry J.
  The constitutional system.

  Includes bibliographies and index.
  1. Legislative power – United States. 2. Executive
power – United States. 3. Separation of powers –
United States. 4. United States – Constitutional law.
I. Title.
KF4930.M47 1986   342.73'044   86-15162
                           347.30244
ISBN 0-275-92185-9 (alk. paper)

Library of Congress Catalog Card Number: 86-15162
ISBN: 0-275-92185-9

First published in 1986

Praeger Publishers, 521 Fifth Avenue, New York, NY 10175
A division of Greenwood Press, Inc.

Printed in the United States of America

The paper used in this book complies with the Permanent
Paper Standard issued by the National Information Standards
Organization (Z39.48-1984).

10 9 8 7 6 5 4 3 2 1

The whole art of statesmanship is the art of bringing the several parts of government into effective cooperation for the accomplishment of particular common objectives.

Woodrow Wilson
Constitutional Government
1908, p. 54.

CONTENTS

PART III:

THE PRESENT STATE OF THE CONSTITUTIONAL SYSTEM

1

Introduction

To study one branch of government in isolation from the others is usually an exercise in make-believe. Very few operations of Congress and the presidency are genuinely independent and autonomous.

Louis Fisher[1]

There is an inherent tension between Congress and the presidency, yet cooperation between the two institutions is necessary if the government is to act in a significant way.

Richard A. Watson and Norman C. Thomas[2]

We find in fact that both Congress and the President share in legislative and executive powers.

Arthur Maass[3]

In the end, both the president and Congress have to recognize that they are not two sides out to "win" but two parts of the same government, both elected to pursue together the interests of the American people.

Thomas E. Cronin[4]

Our constitutional system has been adapting itself to new conditions and forces for 200 years. This study undertakes to explain that the principal change during this period has been in the group character of the House of Representatives, the Senate, and the presidency.

1

THE PUBLIC POLICY SUPERSTRUCTURE

At the start, Congress and the presidency were called legislative and executive powers. Now they are a public policy superstructure with shared functions—above all, representation. This study argues that we should perceive them to be a separate group with common responsibilities. There are several difficulties, however. One is that the Constitution does not deal with them as a group but refers to them as separate entities, a Congress of two houses and a president. Also, the Constitution does not expressly identify the duties of a representational group. Rather, the most prominent provisions of the Constitution explicitly associate Congress with legislative powers and the presidency with executive power.

The overriding difficulty in trying to explain a new perception of this group is that many will continue to think of Congress as legislative and the president as executive even when both are engaged in another type of function.

The transition of Congress and the presidency from separate legal powers to common public policy responsibilities has involved several developments. One has been the considerable fusion of legislation and execution in various fields of operation.[5] Much of this book will explain how Congress and the president exercise common control of both legislation and execution.

The second step toward group character has been the enlargement of the system of representation. At the beginning, only the House was fully representational; the Senate and the president were policy checks upon the House. Now, the latter two are representational—by virtue of a broader meaning of representation as well as official and unofficial changes in selection methods.[6]

Third, representation has been intensified by the increase in the number of states and districts and the greater attention to the constituencies. Also, the national society is now more diversified, with stronger organization of numerous special interests. The growth of public relations has enhanced the conflict among the units seeking special representation.

The major political parties might seem to unify the majority forces in these institutions, but the parties have become weak in spirit and organization. Also, internal divisions may cause each party to have a number of ideological sectors. Moreover, the practice of "split-ticket" voting may result in one or both houses of Congress having a party majority that differs from the party of the White House.[7]

This description of the elected institutions highlights the many separations and conflicts. Can we derive a more positive perception of the group that reflects its common functions? First, we need to identify the representational responsibilities.

COMMON REPRESENTATIONAL DUTIES

Representational responsibilities are not stipulated in the Constitution. We will present an unofficial identification, which divides those relating to the public from those concerning governmental units. The first group includes (a) reconciliation of the three electoral actions of the voters; (b) the integration of conflicts among public interest groups; (c) the development of public policy objectives; (d) the guidance and scrutiny of legislative programs; and (e) the direction of public communication.

The second group includes (a) the integration of policy conflicts among governmental units; (b) the guidance and scrutiny of the appointed officials in the legislative and executive systems; and (c) final action on proposed legislation.

Those two levels of responsibilities are presented in Figure 1, which includes a graphic arrangement of the relationships among the three elected institutions. The pattern has the general lines of a triangle or pyramid, but it is more open than solid. It is not a design of authority but rather a suggestion of working interactions. The president is above, the Senate next, and the House forms the broad foundation. The connecting lines are near center, and they recognize the usual difference between the two major parties. What is most important in this arrangement is that the president is at or near the center and not to the left or right.

Figure 1. The Public Policy Superstructure

Responsibilities in Relation to the Public
Reconciliation of the three electoral messages
Integration of conflicting public interests
Development of national policy objectives
Guidance and scrutiny of legislative programs
Official public communication

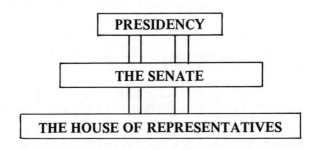

Responsibilities in Relation to the Government
Integration of public interest conflicts
Guidance and scrutiny of appointed officials
in legislative and executive systems
Final action on proposed legislation

THREE LEVELS OF CHECKS AND BALANCES

A constitution is essentially a set of restrictions upon the relevant government. Limitations are of two general types: direct prohibitions, such as the rule against ex post facto criminal laws, and indirect restrictions, such as the checks and balances among separated powers.

History and political science seem to agree that there are two basic patterns of checks and balances in constitutional distributions of power: politically separated institutions having common legal functions, and politically neutral institutions having separated legal functions. The latter may be divided into rigid and flexible types.

The arrangement of politically separated institutions is often called the "mixed constitution."[8] It is as old as political science; in fact, it may have been the start of that art during the classical era in Greece and Rome. It seeks to assure the sharing of high policy making by the one, the few, and the many, or by monocratic, aristocratic, and democratic forces.

The concept of the "mixed constitution" is essentially similar to the formula of "separated institutions *sharing* powers" in Richard Neustadt's 1960 book, *Presidential Power.*[9] That idea has been approved in many textbooks on U.S. national government, but there has been little if any identification of the patterns of arrangement to which it applies. This book suggests that it may help us gain a more positive perception of the group of three elected institutions.

The second pattern emerged from the English Civil War of the 1640s.[10] It involves execution and adjudication as well as policy legislation. The emphasis is upon separate legal functions and in its rigid form seeks to assure an individual accused of crime a fair procedure. American colonists became interested in the criminal procedure in the 1760s when London began stern methods to enforce tax laws and trade regulations.[11] It is prominent in the first U.S. state constitutions and in the U.S. Constitution. The less rigid form of this distribution pattern appears in the vast noncriminal law operations of the government.

This book suggests that the "mixed constitution" or "common functions" pattern provides a positive guide to the group character of the three elected institutions, but we do not apply that formula to the other parts or levels of the government.

We will bring the three patterns of arrangement together in a composite typology by considering them to be different means for gaining the ends of the general principle of checks and balances. We will call the three levels the public policy superstructure, the criminal law infrastructure, and the mixed power middle structure. These three levels of distributed powers will be explained more fully in Chapter 13.

The main point of this larger picture of constitutional limitations is that the concept of separated institutions with common functions, such as representation, gives us a better indication of the group character of the elected institutions than the formula of separate legislative, executive, and judicial functions.

FUNDAMENTAL QUESTIONS

This study of the separate group character of the houses of Congress and the presidency presents a number of basic questions. The principal ones include:

After applying the idea of separating powers for 200 years, should we now start practicing the idea of integrating powers? Have the changes in the election system made the elected institutions a special case in this regard?

Do the elected institutions constitute a separate group? Should that group be designated the "public policy superstructure" or the "representational branch" of the national government?

Has there been substantial fusion of legislative and executive powers? Are Congress and the presidency both responsible for both the legislative and executive systems?

Is the group of three elected institutions an example of separated institutions sharing functions even though the other institutions have separated functions?

Is the pattern of separated legislative, executive, and judicial functions especially protective of individuals accused of crime? Were the American Founders particularly interested in this distribution of governmental powers?

Do the developmental roots of U.S. government include both the "mixed constitution" and the legislative-executive-judicial separation forms of distributed powers? This is considered in Chapter 2 of this study.

At the Constitutional Convention of 1787, was there a basic difference between the "national executive," proposed by the Virginia Plan at the start of the convention, and the "President of the United States," proposed by the draft constitution during the latter part of the convention? This question is dealt with in Chapters 3 and 4.

Does the Constitution give Congress primary control of the executive system and the president a leadership role in the legislative process? Chapters 5 and 6 address this question.

Does the Constitution and its adaptation give the Congress and the presidency common responsibilities in the making of both foreign and domestic policy? This issue is examined in Part II (Chapters 7 through 11).

Have changes in the processes of nomination and election caused the
president and Congress to grow farther apart? Are there three
patterns of separation of powers in support of a general
principle of checks and balances? Are the three elected
institutions obligated to determine a composite public policy
for the public and the government? These questions are considered in Part III.

In summation, the principal objective of this study is to explain a
more positive way of perceiving the relationships of the president
and the houses of Congress in their representation of the national
electorate and in their supervision of the legislative and executive
systems of the national government.

NOTES

1. Louis Fisher, *The Politics of Shared Power: Congress and the Executive*
(Washington, D.C.: Congressional Quarterly Press, 1981), p. xi.
2. Richard A. Watson and Norman C. Thomas, *The Politics of the Presidency* (New York: John Wiley, 1983), p. 245.
3. Arthur Maass, *Congress and the Common Good* (New York: Basic Books,
1983), p. 13.
4. Thomas E. Cronin, *The State of the Presidency*, 2d ed. (Boston: Little,
Brown, 1980), p. 220.
5. See, in general, Louis W. Koenig, *Congress and the President* (Chicago:
Scott, Foresman, 1965) and Nelson W. Polsby, *Congress and the Presidency*, 4th
ed. (Englewood Cliffs, N.J.: Prentice-Hall, 1980). See also books in notes 1-4.
6. "The American presidency was not designed to be the center of leadership in the new republic. . . . The alchemy of time transformed the role of the
President into what has more recently been called the imperial and even the om-
nipotent presidency." James MacGregor Burns, *Leadership* (New York: Harper &
Row, 1978), p. 385. On today's presidency, see Clinton Rossiter, *The American
Presidency*, rev. ed. (New York: New American Library, 1956), pp. 251-52;
Benjamin I. Page and Mark P. Petracca, *The American Presidency* (New York:
McGraw-Hill, 1983); and Erwin C. Hargrove and Michael Nelson, *Presidents,
Politics, and Policy* (Baltimore: Johns Hopkins University Press, 1984).
7. For instance, during the 34 years 1953-87, the Republicans held the
White House for 22 years, but only in the first two (1953-55) of these years did
the Republicans have a majority in both houses of Congress. The Democrats held
the White House for 12 years and had a majority in both houses during all 12 of
these years.
8. Kurt von Fritz, *The Theory of the Mixed Constitution in Antiquity*
(New York: Columbia University Press, 1954). See the section entitled "The
Classical Concept of High Policy Interdependence" in chapter 2.

9. Richard Neustadt, *Presidential Power: The Politics of Leadership* (New York: Wiley, 1960), p. 33 (1980 ed., p. 26).

10. Francis D. Wormuth, *The Origins of Modern Constitutionalism* (New York: Harper & Bros., 1949), pp. 59-70; William Gwyn, *The Meaning of Separation of Powers* (New Orleans: Tulane University Press, 1967), p. 28-65; M. J. C. Vile, *Constitutionalism and the Separation of Powers* (Oxford: Clarendon Press, 1967), pp. 39-51.

11. Paul Merrill Spurlin, *Montesquieu in America 1760-1801* (University: Louisiana State University Press, 1940), p. 99.

PART I

FORMATION OF
THE CONSTITUTIONAL SYSTEM

THE START OF THE REPRESENTATIONAL PYRAMID

An appraisal of the 200-year change in the separate group character of the houses of Congress and the presidency involves an understanding of the role of these institutions when the constitutional system began, as well as their responsibilities today. The Constitution gives prominence to the separation of both functions and institutions, and we need to assess the importance attached to those separations at the time of our sovereign establishment.

For these reasons, Part I will concern the formation of the constitutional system. Four of its five chapters will analyze the proceedings at the Constitutional Convention and the treatment of the Congress and the president in the Constitution. These chapters will be preceded by a chapter that analyzes the constitutional principles and practices at that time.

Chapter 2 will review the principal developmental roots of U.S. government with particular emphasis upon the classical doctrine of the mixed constitution, bringing together democratic, aristocratic, and monocratic forces, and upon the more modern pattern of separate legislative, executive, and judicial functions.

Chapters 3 and 4 will review the Constitutional Covnvention of 1787. Their separate treatment of the two parts of the convention is of particular significance. The first part concerns the Virginia Plan and the national infrastructure, while the second relates to the mid-convention draft constitution and the potentials of the tripartite superstructure for public policy determination.

Chapters 5 and 6 will analyze the constitutional provisions relating to the Congress and the presidency, respectively. The stress here will be upon the potentials of these institutions for common responsibilities with respect to the legislative, executive, and representational processes.

2

Developmental Roots of U.S. Government

What is of primary importance is to prevent the legislative power from being abused, and that can only be done by making king, lords, and commons share in its exercise.
                                        Carl J. Friedrich and Robert G. McCloskey[1]

The American constitutions of the eighteenth century gave great attention to the protection of persons accused of crime.
                                        Francis D. Wormuth[2]

Just as Americans continued to be suspicious of governors even when they were elective, so they continued to be suspicious of central authority even when it was their own.
                                        Edmund S. Morgan[3]

"Governmental institutions grow; they are not invented overnight."[4] Joseph Kallenbach, in his book on chief executives, says this of the presidency, but it is equally, and probably more, appropriate with respect to representative assemblies, councils, courts, congresses, and specialized administrators.

An "evolutionary process" began, he says, with the founding of the first English colony here in 1607.[5] That was 380 years ago. The Constitution of 1787 came at nearly the midpoint of our political experience on this continent.

There are distinguishable antecedents for both the superstructure and infrastructure patterns of constitutional arrangement. The im-

13

mediate precedents for the first were the English Parliament of the king, the House of Lords, and the House of Commons and the colonial system of governor, council, and assembly.[6] Likewise, the ordered sequence of legislative, executive, and judicial functions may be found in the English criminal law tradition.[7]

THE CLASSICAL CONCEPT OF
HIGH POLICY INTERDEPENDENCE

If there is a wisdom of the ages in governmental and political theory, it is the ancient Greek and Roman idea of the "mixed constitution."[8] That is a form of tripartite superstructure that checks power with power. It assumes that there are three kinds of government—monarchy, aristocracy, and democracy—and that each, when left to itself alone, tends to degenerate into a bad form, such as despotism or oligarchy. Classical theorists argued that if a government embodied three such institutions they would mutually check excess and degeneration.[9]

The tripartite pattern appears not only in philosophies and histories but also in early literature. At the start of Homer's *Odyssey*, there are indications that the government of Ithaca was designed to include a king, a council, and an assembly.[10]

Sparta probably had the most continuously mixed constitution. It combined a duplex royalty, a small group of *ephors* (censors or auditors of a sort), and a senate and an assembly.[11] The same form is supposed to have continued for eight centuries. Athens had a more open system when it was not under the arm of a tyrant. Its first democratic period began in 510 B.C. Its most democratic period was 460–430 B.C. That system combined an assembly of citizens, or *Ecclesia,* a small continuing council, or *Aeropagus,* and a panel of elected generals.[12] Pericles, scion of an old liberal family, was re-elected a general each year. He appears to have been the Athenian version of a "patriot king."

The assembly of citizens, in both Sparta and Athens, had limited legislative authority. At least on important questions, it had the final word only on measures presented by an elite panel. At those times, the assembly could vote yes, no, or try again.[13] Thus, there is early precedent for the conciliar guidance of the democratic assembly or, in general for presidential proposal and congressional disposal of political legislation.

The leading Athenian philosophers had particular explanations of the elements that resulted in the best combination of action and political liberty. Plato's *Laws* suggest that a government should have some aspects of both monarchy and democracy.[14] Then, Aristotle's *Politics* combines oligarchy and democracy for the best way to reach the ideal of government by a large middle class.[15] Later writers also esteemed the mixed constitution. Polybius, the Greek noble who became a Roman historian about 150 B.C., found the pattern in the Roman Republic. He described the two military consuls as the monarchical element, the Senate as aristocratic, and the people as democratic.[16] Polybius also elaborated the theory that simple forms result in revolution. Later, Cicero, in his *Republic,* calls the combination of monarchy, aristocracy, and democracy the best government. St. Thomas Aquinas, the great Dominican theologian, writing in the thirteenth century, made a similar assertion. Also, he suggested that this had been the type of government prescribed by Moses for the Israelites.[17]

The influence of classical thought upon the modern era is evident in the writing of the English republican theorist James Harrington. In 1656 he wrote when Cromwell had replaced the kings of England:

> Government, according to the ancients and their learned disciple Machiavelli (the only politician of later ages), is of three kinds: the government of one man, or of the better sort, or of the whole people, which by their more learned names are called monarchy, aristocracy, and democracy.
>
> These they hold, through their proneness to degenerate, to be all evil. . . . Wherefore, as reason and passion are two things, so government by reason is one thing and the corruption of government by passion is another thing; . . .
>
> The corruption, then, of monarchy is called tyranny; that of aristocracy, oligarchy; and that of democracy, anarchy. But legislators, having found these three governments at best to be nought, have invented another consisting of a mixture of them all, which only is good. This is the doctrine of the ancients.[18]

Later, Harrington applies the classical idea of mixed constitution to the conditions of seventeenth century England and gives us this pattern of tripartite government:

> Wherefore as those two orders of a commonwealth, namely the senate and the people, are *legislative,* so of necessity there must be a

third to be *executive* of the laws made, and this is the magistracy; in which order with the rest being wrought up by art, the commonwealth consists of the senate proposing, the people resolving, and the magistracy executing.

Whereby, partaking of the aristocracy as in the senate, of the democracy as in the people, and of monarchy as in the magistracy, it is complete. Now there being no other commonwealth but this in art or nature, it is no wonder if Machiavelli has showed us that the ancients held this only to be good.[19]

The institutions identified here are similar to those in Montesquieu's explanation of "the fundamental constitution" in his chapter on the English system, that is, the two branches of the legislature and the monarch.[20]

The English government was unbalanced during the period 1630-60 with the king, the Commons, and a military protector, each trying to rule alone for about a decade. But after the restoration of the Stuart monarchy in 1660, there was a period of "balanced constitution." The king, the Lords, and the Commons had about the same strength, and the three tended to balance each other. In 1688 Parliament forced a change in the monarchy, and the theory of legislative supremacy took hold.

This was expressed in the essays of John Locke, an empirical philosopher with much influence in England, America, and France. Locke's *Second Treatise on Government* (about 1690) gives us three patterns of constitutional arrangement. First, he sets forth a sequence of legislative, judicial, and executive powers, as if the executive serves to enforce the judicial decrees. Later, he says that the three powers are legislative, federative, and executive. The second pattern concerns foreign affairs and the third the judiciary. Then, in the last chapter of the *Treatise* he recognizes a legislature with the following elements:

1. A single hereditary Person having the constant, supreme, executive Power, and with it the Power of Convoking and Dissolving the other two within certain Periods of time;
2. An Assembly of Hereditary Nobility;
3. An Assembly of Representatives chosen *pro tempore,* by the People;[21]

The contribution of the tripatrite legislature to constitutional limitation is quite evident in the analysis of the English government by the great legal scholar William Blackstone in the 1760s. This, of course, was after *The Spirit of the Laws* was published, but it makes clear the contribution of this arrangement. Blackstone's explanation includes these observations:

> And herein indeed consists the true excellence of the English government, that all parts of it form a mutual check upon each other. In the legislature, the people are a check upon the nobility, and the nobility a check upon the people; by the mutual privilege of rejecting what the other has resolved: while the king is a check upon both, which preserves the executive power from encroachments.
>
> And this very executive power is again checked, and kept within due bounds by the two houses, through the privilege they have of enquiring into, impeaching, and punishing the conduct (not indeed of the king, which would destroy his constitutional independence; but, which is more beneficial to the public) of his evil and pernicious counsellors.
>
> Thus every branch of our civil polity supports and is supported, regulates and is regulated, by the rest; . . . Like three distinct powers in mechanics, they jointly impel the machine of government in a direction different from what either, acting by themselves, would have done; but . . . a direction which constitutes the true line of liberty. . . . [22]

The English Parliament of king, Lords, and Commons was not established in response to a theory; it developed over centuries in response to conflicting political pressures. Its antecedents include the practice of English kings, begun even before the coming of the Normans, to consider the advice of a council. In feudal times the council included the great barons. The Magna Carta was the settlement of a dispute between the king and the barons. Even within its actual limits, the charter is a precedent for the political reconciliation of high-level conflicts.

Quite often, the king had two councils, a small one and a large one. In some degree, those two led to the two houses of Parliament, the Lords and the Commons. In contrast, Louis XIII, Louis XIV, and Louis XV usually did not consult a council but acted through a single figure, such as Cardinal Richelieu. That may have been the basis of Montesquieu's preference for the English system.

Change continued even after Parliament became three separate forces. During the seventeenth century, the kings encountered a series of reversals. Later, the connection between the king's ministers and the Commons grew closer. Still later, ministers gained support of the Commons through patronage and extra means, or at times the Commons controlled the ministers through party affiliation. What was happening was often not clear, and the significance of developments was obscure. Eventually this became the present parliamentary-cabinet system, but that was not evident at the time.

FUNCTIONAL INTERDEPENDENCE OF CRIMINAL LAW PROCESSES

Developments in England during the American colonial period concerned not only the distribution of power among the high-level *institutions,* that is, the kings, the Lords, and the Commons, but also the separation of legislative, executive, and judicial *functions* in the system of law enforcement.

There were two landmark developments during the English Civil War. First, there was the abolition in 1641 of the Court of the Star Chamber, which had been notoriously dominated by the king's Privy Council and had exercised a nonjury inquisitorial procedure.[23] Its abolition allowed enforcement processes to abide by the accepted rules including a fair judicial trial.

Then, later in the 1640s, when the House of Commons sought to rule by itself, there were attempts by that body to try its political enemies, such as John Lilburne, the head of the radical "Levelers," and the king, Charles I, for criminal offenses.

In this, the Commons went beyond acknowledged practices, such as impeachment of the king's ministers, or the adoption of bills of attainder against individual citizens or officials. It undertook to hold trials directly or through its appointed commissions. For instance, the Commons in 1645 called Lilburne before its Committee on Examinations for his refusal to take the Covenant Oath. Later, the House of Commons had its Council of State imprison and interrogate Lilburne. Lilburne claimed that he was entitled to a hearing under settled rules of law rather than by arbitrary process. He also asserted that the Commons had no authority to act as a trial court. The debates on this invoked the idea of the separation of legislative, executive, and judicial functions.[24]

There may be some confusion in the arguments because at the time the term *executive* was used to include judicial as well as administrative functions, even though in substance and practice the judiciary was independent of the executive in its more limited sense. The assertions may have been for separation of legislative and executive functions, but the intent was separation of trial procedure from the functions of the House of Commons.

Francis D. Wormuth, in his scholarly book on the origins of modern constitutionalism, states that "the first purpose for which the separation of the legislative and executive powers" was advocated was "to insure that accused persons be tried by the known procedure of courts of justice" and that they be "convicted by settled rules previously enacted," rather than by the policy considerations of a legislative body.[25]

Other leading scholars of the origin of the principle of separate powers seem to agree that the doctrine emerged in the political and constitutional debates of the English Civil War of the 1640s.[26] The contentions of Lilburne became modern constitutional principles, which are guaranteed in the Fifth and Sixth Amendments to the Constitution of the United States.

Since the crucial developments in English constitutional law and practice during the seventeenth century, at least the following separation of powers in England has been maintained: that the House of Commons cannot try an individual person for violation of a criminal statute. The Fifth and Sixth Amendments to our Constitution have their roots in the constitutional law of England as well as expressing our own fundamental limitations.

There, Montesquieu seems to be right in his conclusion about the political liberty of the subject or citizen in England. Moreover, it will be seen that that is where he was most appreciated by the American colonists who faced stern English processes after 1762. The practice of quoting Montesquieu in letters to newspaper editors started when London began to use "writs of assistance" and to try Americans in the admiralty court, with its denial of a jury trial.[27]

CONGRESSES OF THE AMERICAN FOUNDING PERIOD

Many nations have been founded by military or monarchical systems, but the founding of the United States of America was guided by a series of congresses in which representation was by colony or state. After 1760 they protested London actions.

One protest Congress gathered in 1765 in reaction to the 1763 reorganization of the British Empire and the imposition of the Stamp Tax for raising revenue among the colonies. That Congress asserted such fundamental principles as the entitlement of colonists to the "inherent rights and liberties" of British subjects.[28]

The more forceful and most continuous efforts came with the First Continental Congress of 1774 and the second one of 1775-81. The latter served added years because of the delay in the acceptance of the Articles of Confederation. They were drafted in 1777 but did not take effect until 1781 because of disputes over the status of western lands.

The two Continental Congresses issued proclamations in 1774, 1775, and 1776 that expressed the American protests against the authorities in London. The first two were directed at the Parliament while the last—and most noted—one attacked the king himself and in fact broke the legal and political ties with the sovereign.

The Second Continental Congress urged the separate states to establish provisional or permanent governments. The charter colonies, Connecticut and Rhode Island, renamed their basic laws. The other 11 colony-states, acting largely through their legislatures, adopted constitutions. New Hampshire and South Carolina had temporary ones for a year to two. There were eight new constitutions in 1776 and 1777 and three later.

The next section of this chapter will review the extent to which the new state constitutions embodied policy superstructures, such as a representative assembly, a senate, and a governor.

Then, two sections will analyze the Articles of Confederation, with particular consideration of the division of sovereignty between the central authority and the states. The articles' principal operating deficiency was their lack of internal sovereignty.

HIGH POLICY INTERDEPENDENCE IN THE NEW STATE GOVERNMENTS[29]

The United States began its independent life in 1776 with its national sovereignty divided. The external sovereignty, including the authority to conduct foreign relations, passed to the union of states as a single entity. That sovereignty was exercised by the Continental Congresses until 1781. Then it was exercised by the Congress of the Confederation until the new Constitution went into effect.

The internal sovereignty passed severally to the 13 new states. Each state had within its territory the sole authority to tax and regulate individual persons and to impose criminal punishment. The Articles of Confederation expressly recognized that sovereignty was in the states. The Constitution of 1787 did not mention "sovereignty," but its effect was to nationalize a substantial portion of the internal sovereignty.

The legislatures of the new states acted rather promptly in 1776 to draft and then to put into effect new constitutions. The two "charter" colonies, Connecticut and Rhode Island, had been largely independent before the Revolution. They simply retitled their charters.

The other states, mostly acting through their legislatures, adopted new constitutions. New Hampshire and South Carolina had temporary constitutions in 1776 and later adopted more final ones. The other new states adopted what were deemed to be permanent constitutions. Among the 11 states, 6 adopted constitutions in 1776, 2 in 1777, and 1 each in 1778, 1780, and 1784.

Seven states led by their respective legislatures adopted separate comprehensive bills of rights. These states were Virginia, Delaware, Maryland, North Carolina, and Pennsylvania in 1776, Massachusetts in 1780, and New Hampshire in 1784. Virginia and Massachusetts were leaders in this regard, and there was much similarity in the rights declared in these addenda to the respective constitutions. Other states stipulated a number of rights in their constitutions proper.

The colonial experience of the Americans is evident in the institutional pattern of the new constitutions. Each state established a representative assembly with apparently the expectation that it would protect or serve the community as the assemblies generally had done in the colonial period.

The attachment of the constitution makers in the states to the idea of mixed representation and counterbalanced legislative process is evident in their readiness to provide for second legislative chambers, such as a senate. A single chamber could have met the legislative needs of the doctrine of separate legislative, executive, and judicial powers. Moreover, the historical precedents for a senate were not attractive. The Roman senate had been oligarchic, the House of

Lords was still largely hereditary, and the colonial councils often had been agents of the governors in the exertion of pressure upon the representative assemblies and even upon the courts. Despite these unfavorable factors, most of the state constitutions provided for a senate or other second chamber.

Georgia and Pennsylvania were the only states in which the constitution did not provide for two legislative institutions, but each did prescribe an executive council. In Georgia the elected representatives chose the council from their own number, with each major county being represented. Pennsylvania was also unusual because it was the only state without a governor or other single executive chief. Pennsylvania had a 12-man executive council, the members of which were elected by the voters. The presiding officer of this council was entitled "president," but the position was more like that of a present-day chairman of the board rather than that of the executive president of a present-day corporation.

Ten of the eleven new constitutions embodied the institutional pattern of the classical mixed government, with only the one exception for the truncated structure in Pennsylvania. In general, there was a superstructure of the one, the few, and the many. That design, we have emphasized, is uppermost in the government of the United States today. The nation and 49 states have three power representation and legislation. Only Nebraska does not have a senate.

The most interesting development in the new constitutions, from the viewpoint of this book, was the "politicizing" of the governor (or in three states, the president). This development is evident in three main respects. One is the general introduction of short terms for governors. Comparatively short terms for representative legislators had become almost a tradition in England and a common practice in the American colonies. But executive officials had served for life, or for the pleasure of the monarch. In contrast, the governors of the new states had terms of three years or less. In fact, a one-year term was the most common.

The second development that tended to increase the political character of the chief executives concerned the method of selection. There was, of course, no hereditary dynasty or nobility for determining the monarch, prime minister, or council, for either executive, administrative, or appointive functions. The majority of the governors or state presidents were chosen by the respective state legislatures, which were definitely political-minded bodies. Three constitutions (New York, Massachusetts, and New Hampshire) called for selection by citizen ballots. The long-range trend probably was toward popular selection. We will see that in the national government the popular election of the president was virtually complete by 1828, 40 years after the adoption of the new Constitution. But even selection by state legislatures or by an electoral college system with popular, or semipopular choice of electors, has some element of political selection or responsibility.

The third factor affecting the political character of governors or other "chief executives" was the declarations in some bills of rights bracketing executive officials with legislative ones in the contrast of political and judicial figures. Present-day analysts often find a political element in judicial decision making, but in the eighteenth century both the colonial and the state charters assumed or asserted a basic distinction between "political" and judicial offices.

The Virginia Bill of Rights seems outstanding in this particular. The Virginia Constitution proper declared that legislative, executive, and judicial departments ought to be separate. Then the Bill of Rights set forth another separation principle, which provided that "the legislative and executive powers of the state should be separate and distinct from the judiciary."[30] This seems to reflect a belief that government by the consent of the people entails frequent elections. The differentiation of legislative and executive officials, on the one hand, and judicial officers, on the other, was part of the proposition that the former "may be restrained from oppression" by being "reduced to a private station" at fixed periods. This meant frequent and regular elections.

The idea of short terms for executive officials, we have noted, was one of the principal contributions of the American independence movement to modern constitutional theory and practice. Likewise, the right to frequent, periodic elections of representatives, even as often as every year, seems to have been the U.S. answer to such guarantees as inalienable individual rights, natural law, deposition, or revolution. Certain assured elections every year are an easier and more dependable device than impeachment, recall, judicial or other trial, or even declarations of unconstitutionality.

The declarations, such as the one in the Virginia Bill of Rights, also demonstrate the separate dependence upon the traditional judicial system. Each of the new state constitutions of 1776–84 established a judicial system with the Anglo-American procedure and methods, such as trial by jury. The state bills of rights also sought to protect individual rights to fair and just criminal law procedure.

The declarations that "political" officials should be subject to frequent elections imply a general belief that the judges were sufficiently responsible to the law and also that the law was sufficiently fair and firm that the frequent election or reelection of judges was not necessary.

The majority of the state constitutions of 1776–84 followed the English developments in giving judges definite security of tenure. Seven of the 11 new constitutions prescribed terms of "good behavior" (or usually life), and the other states stipulated terms of at least five years. In contrast, no state legislative or executive official had a term of more than five years, and many had only one-year terms. The longest nonjudicial terms were for senators in Maryland (five years) and New York and Virginia (four years).

One aspect of the state constitutions that may bear upon the role of the president under the national constitution of 1787 is the extent to which the state governors were designated to be "commanders in chief" of the military forces of the respective states. The common belief is that the governors of 1776 were "weak." They had little veto power, and their appointive power often was limited by a council or other means. However, each of the governors (or state presidents) was given the headship of the state militia. In some states the legislatures or a council were involved in the action of calling out the militia. The governors, however, had command of the militia after it was called. Moreover, 9 of the 11 new constitutions used the term *commander in chief* in assigning the duty over the state militia. Thus that term had much association with "weak" governors and may not have carried great power or expectation when applied by the national Constitution of 1787 to the office of the president.

DISTRIBUTION PATTERN OF
THE ARTICLES OF CONFEDERATION

A central government for the 13 new states was proposed in 1777 but, because of a dispute over the control of western lands, was not adopted until 1781.[31] The Articles of Confederation established a union of states rather than of people. They acknowledged that each state retained its "sovereignty, freedom and independence" and that the Congress of the Confederation had powers only "expressly declared." They made no explicit claim to "external sovereignty," but most of their delegated powers concerned foreign affairs and interstate comity.

The articles provided for a Congress with equal representation from each state. The Congress was much like an international council with delegates acting for the member states. When the Congress was not in session, a Committee of States, with one member from each member state could act on matters of secondary importance. The Congress could appoint officials, and we will see that when it began official operation in 1781 it established three departments, each with a single head, in the areas of foreign affairs, finance, and military matters.[32]

The powers expressly granted to the Congress concerned mostly foreign affairs. The list of authorizations is perhaps most important because they were the basis for the extensive grants of power over external matters to Congress in the Constitution of 1787. The Articles of Confederation did provide some authority over commercial matters, such as determining the value of currency, and the standard of weights and measures throughout the United States. However, the large proportion of powers dealt with security matters and foreign affairs, such as:

> The sole and exclusive right and power of determining on peace and war, except in case of invasion,
> Sending and receiving ambassadors,
> Entering into treaties or alliances [excluding restraints on commerce],
> Establishing rules for deciding in all cases what captures on land or water shall be legal, . . .
> Granting letters of marque and reprisal in times of peace;
> Appointing courts for the trial of piracies and felonies committed on the high seas, . . .
> Appointing all officers of the land forces, . . .
> Appointing all the officers of the naval forces, . . .
> Making rules for the government and regulation of the said land and naval forces, and directing their operation.

Most of these powers, as will be seen, were later granted to Congress in the 1787 Constitution.

The extensive grants of foreign affairs authority to Congress show how far the esteem of legislative assemblies had grown during the preceding 100 years. In the 1680s the English philosopher John Locke asserted in his famous *Second Treatise on Civil Government* that "the power of war and peace, leagues and alliances," and all external transactions, constitute a "federative" power to be handled by the executive. Locke's argument was that such matters "are much less capable to be directed by antecedent, standing, positive laws."[33]

Now in the newly independent U.S. states, the "founders" definitely assigned such matters to Congress. Moreover, the Constitution of 1787 enlarged the powers of Congress in this area, even authorizing Congress to declare "offenses against the law of nations." Thus the Constitution makers assumed that such matters could be dealt with by antecedent, standing, positive laws. This demonstrates the substantial growth of confidence in the control power of statutory law during the century between the English and American revolutions.

Some analysts of the Confederation period seem to assume that the committee of state delegates was the only operational or executive structure. As a matter of fact, the Congress established in 1781 three single-headed departments, as described by a leading historian of the period:

> In January 1781, a Department of Foreign Affairs was created and in February the departments of Finance and War, each to be run by one man who would be responsible to Congress and hold office during its pleasure.
>
> ... the very existence of secretaries whose sole business was to administer a department and who could be held responsible for its activities was a considerable advance in the creation of an effective national government. Each department developed a small staff of workers who became the first professional civil servants of the United States and in many cases continued to work in the same capacities under the new government after the Confederation ended.[34]

The Department of Finance was headed by Robert Morris, a strong-minded administrator. In fact, he was so strong that when the war ended he was replaced by a committee of three. John Jay was in charge of foreign affairs during the final years of the Confederation. He served as secretary of state at the start of Washington's presidency for nearly a year until Thomas Jefferson was able to begin. Jay apparently dominated the congressional consideration of foreign relations. Wilfred Binkley in his history of Congress and the presidency calls Jay the "Chief Executive of the Government" at the time of his service to the Confederation.[35]

Henry Knox, a leading general of the Independence War, headed the War Department during the final four years of the Confederation and then during the first four years under the Constitution of 1787. Some of the professional staff also served during the two periods. For example, Joseph Nourse was registrar of the treasury from 1781 to 1829.

The existence of these three departments and the post office at the time that the Constitutional Convention met in 1787 is probably why the delegations assumed but did not authorize the establishment of departments. Apparently, they believed that Congress would continue the departmental structures under its more general authorizations. In fact, that is what Congress did as soon as it met in 1789.

The only new department established when the Constitution of 1787 went into effect in 1789 was the Office of the Attorney-General. It was not called a department until well into the next century, but the attorney general was a member of President Washington's cabinet. The fact that this was the only new executive establishment immediately answerable to the president is further indication that the principal change in 1789 was the power to enforce obligations with respect to taxes, regulations, and other coercive matters.

NEED FOR PARTIAL NATIONALIZATION
OF INTERNAL SOVEREIGNTY

During the years after the Independence War, and particularly during 1786 and 1787, when some of the more national-minded of the political activists in the larger states were proposing a convention to amend the Articles of Confederation, the inadequacies of the Confederation government were increasingly apparent.

There were instances of weakness among the state governments. For instance, in 1786 debtor farmers in western Massachusetts turned to forceful protest against the state authorities. Shays's Rebellion was not large nor long lasting, but it did disturb the middle class as well as the financial aristocracy.[36]

The principal difficulties were with the central government. The difficulties encountered by the Confederation Congress in its lack of funds and its problems of enforcement have been described.

The operation of the national institutions of the Confederation system had considerable effect upon the aims and actions of the Constitutional Convention. The experiences were both positive and negative. Present-day analysts of the U.S. national government are much occupied with the relations of the president and Congress, and when they look back upon the Confederation period the absence of a presidential-type official seems to be the major, if not the sole, defect of that arrangement. Yet the major difficulty was not in the relations of the Congress and what there was of a national executive, but rather it was in the relations of the national institutions as a group with the several state governments.

The Articles of Confederation did not provide specifically for executive departments, but they did authorize the Congress to appoint "civil officers." In 1781, as noted earlier, Congress did establish departments for foreign affairs, finance, and the military. In general, each department functioned with a single head. In the final years, a three-man commission directed the financial department.

The operation of the departments apparently was so satisfactory that the convention of 1787 assumed that they would be continued under the new Constitution. It made no explicit authorization of departments, but the new Congress, largely under its power to enact "necessary and proper" laws, established the three departments anew with only minor adjustments.

The major deficiency of the Confederation system was not its pattern of executive institutions but its lack of internal sovereignty. It had no authority to impose and collect taxes or to take other coercive measures against individuals within the states.[37] Its reliance upon contributions or other action by the state governments was not satisfactory.

Attempts to remedy its lack of taxing power by an amendment to the Articles of Confederation failed because amendments required unanimous consent. In 1782 Rhode Island objected and in 1786 New York held out.[38] If amendments had required only three-fourths approval, as they do now, there might not have been a Constitutional Convention in 1787.[39]

The new Constitution, we will see, resulted in a partial nationalization of the internal sovereignty of the United States. The new Congress had authority to tax, regulate, and even punish.[40]

NOTES

1. Carl J. Friedrich and Robert G. McCloskey, eds., *From the Declaration of Independence to the Constitution: The Roots of American Constitutionalism* (New York: Liberal Arts Press, 1954), p. xiv.

2. Francis D. Wormuth, *The Origins of Modern Constitutionalism* (New York: Harper & Bros., 1949), p. 4.

3. Edmund S. Morgan, *The Birth of the Republic 1763-1789* (Chicago: University of Chicago Press, 1956), p. 105.

4. Joseph Kallenbach, *The American Chief Executive* (New York: Harper & Row., 1966), p. 1.

5. Ibid. "One grand theme runs through all three centuries of American constitutional history. It is the idea of limited government, or what Professor C. H. McIlwain has called 'constitutionalism.' The doctrine of limited government holds that government should proceed within the authority of established institutions and laws, that governmental authority should be limited and defined by law, and that governmental officials should be responsible to law." Alfred H. Kelly and Winfred A. Harbison, *The American Constitution: Its Origins and Development,* 4th ed. (New York: Norton, 1970), p. 6.

6. "For while Parliament was winning control in England, the colonial assemblies were winning it overseas and had tamed the royal governors almost as effectively as Parliament had tamed the King. . . . The supremacy of Parliament had thus become associated in the colonial mind with the supremacy of the assemblies. Both stood for English liberty, for laws made by consent of the people." Morgan, *Birth of the Republic,* p. 12.

7. Wormuth, *Origins of Modern Constitutionalism,* pp. 59-70; William Gwyn, *The Meaning of Separation of Powers* (New Orleans: Tulane University Press, 1967), pp. 28-65; M. J. C. Vile, *Constitutionalism and the Separation of Powers* (Oxford: Clarendon Press, 1967), pp. 39-51.

8. "No part of ancient political theory has had a greater influence on political theory and practice in modern times than the theory of the mixed constitution. . . . to determine what 'mixed constitution' means . . . one must first describe the simple constitutions of which it is supposed to be a mixture. A monarchy . . . , an oligarchy . . . , and a democracy. . . . A mixed constitution, then, by definition is a system in which the supreme power is shared by, and more or less equally distributed among, these three elements." Kurt von Fritz, *The Theory of the Mixed Constitution in Antiquity* (New York: Columbia University Press, 1954), pp. v, 184.

9. Ibid., pp. 60-61, 76, 77; Sir Ernest Barker, *Greek Political Theory* (London: Methuen, 1918), p. 290; T. A. Sinclair, *A History of Greek Political Thought* (London: Routledge & Kegan Paul, 1951), pp. 190, 271-75.

10. *The Odyssey of Homer,* trans. Richmond Lattimore (New York: Harper & Row, 1965), pp. 27, 39. According to J. B. Bury, "The Homeric poems . . . show us the King at the head. But he does not govern wholly on his own will; he is guided by a Council of the chief men of the community whom he consults; and the decisions of the Council and the King deliberating together are brought before the Assembly of the whole people. Out of these three elements—King, Council, Assembly—the constitutions of Europe have grown; here are the germs

of all the various forms of monarchy, aristocracy, and democracy." J. B. Bury, *A History of Greece* (New York: Modern Library, Random House, 1927), pp. 44-45.

11. Bury, *History of Greece*, pp. 114-18; Sinclair, *Greek Political Thought*, pp. 188-91.

12. Bury, *History of Greece*, pp. 200-5, 332-36; David Greene, *Greek Political Theory* (Chicago: University of Chicago Press, 1950), pp. 35-42; Barker, *Greek Political Theory*, pp. 24-36.

13. In his analysis of Sparta, Bury states, "The Council prepared matters which were to come before the Assembly; . . . The Assembly did not debate, but having heard the proposals of kings or ephors, signified its will by acclamation. If it seemed doubtful to which opinion the majority of the voices inclined, recourse was had to a division." With regard to Athens, Bury says, "No proposal could come before the Ecclesia unless it had already been proposed and considered in the Council. Every law passed in the Ecclesia was first sent down from the Council in the form of a *probuleuma*, and, on receiving a majority of votes in the Ecclesia, became a *psephisma.*" Bury, *History of Greece*, pp. 116, 203.

14. Plato, *Laws*, bk. 6, p. 757. Glenn R. Morrow, *Plato's Cretan City: A Historical Interpretation of the Laws* (Princeton: Princeton University Press, 1960), pp. 521-43.

15. Aristotle, *Politics*, bk. 4, pp. viii-xvi; Sinclair, *Greek Political Thought*, pp. 225-29; Sir Ernest Barker, *The Political Thought of Plato and Aristotle* (New York: Dover, 1946), pp. 471-84.

16. Von Fritz, *Mixed Constitution in Antiquity*, pp. 193-219.

17. Cicero, *De re Publica, de Legibus* (Cambridge, Mass.: Harvard University Press, 1928), p. 151. Saint Thomas Aquinas, *Summa Theologia* I-II, Q.cv *Basic Writings of Saint Thomas Aquinas*, vol. 2 (New York: Random House, 1945), pp. 927-28.

18. Charles Blitzer, ed., *The Political Writings of James Harrington* (New York: Liberal Arts Press, 1955), p. 43.

19. Ibid., p. 61.

20. "Here, then, is the fundamental constitution of the government we are treating of. The legislative body being composed of two parts, they check one another by the mutual privilege of rejecting. They are both restrained by the executive power, as the executive is by the legislative." Baron de Montesquieu, *The Spirit of the Laws*, (New York: Hafner, 1949) vol. 1, p. 160 (XI, 6, 55).

21. Peter Laslett, ed., *Locke's Two Treatises of Government* (Cambridge: University Press, 1960), p. 426 (par. 213).

22. William Blackstone, *Commentaries on the Laws of England*, bk. 1 (Oxford: Clarendon Press, 1765), pp. 150-51.

23. Colin R. Lovell, *English Constitutional and Legal History* (New York: Oxford University Press, 1962), p. 317.

24. The account of this development of practice and theory is based upon Wormuth, *Origins of Modern Constitutionalism*, pp. 59-85.

25. Ibid., p. 64.

26. Ibid., pp. 59-70; Gwyn, *Separation of Powers*, pp. 28-65; Vile, *Separation of Powers*, pp. 39-51.

27. Paul Merrill Spurlin, *Montesquieu in America 1760-1801* (University: Louisiana State University Press, 1940), p. 99.

28. "Resolutions of the Stamp Act Congress, October 19, 1765," in Henry Steele Commager, ed., *Documents of American History,* 5th ed. (New York: Appleton-Century-Crofts, 1949), pp. 57, 58.

29. This section is based upon analyses of the constitutions of 1776-84 in Benjamin Perley Poore, ed., *The Federal and State Constitutions, Colonial Charters, and other Organic Laws of the United States* (Washington, D.C.: Government Printing Office, 1877), pp. 273-78, 377-83, 817-28, 1310-14, 1328-29, 1409-14, 1540-48, 1616-27, 1908-12.

30. Ibid., p. 1920.

31. Morgan, *Birth of the Republic,* pp. 101-12; Kelly and Harbison, *American Constitution,* p. 101.

32. Morgan, *Birth of the Republic,* pp. 123-25; Wilfred Binkley, *President and Congress* (New York: Knopf), p. 28.

33. Laslett, *Locke's Two Treatises,* pp. 382-84.

34. Morgan, *Birth of the Republic,* pp. 124-25.

35. Binkley, *President and Congress,* p. 28.

36. Kelly and Harbison, *American Constitution,* p. 109.

37. Alpheus T. Mason and William M. Beaney, *American Constitutional Law,* 5th ed. (Englewood Cliffs, N.J.: Prentice-Hall, 1972), p. 263; C. Herman Pritchett, *The American Constitutional System,* 5th ed. (New York: McGraw-Hill, 1981), p. 15.

38. Morgan, *Birth of the Republic,* p. 126.

39. Benjamin F. Wright, Jr., "The Early History of Written Constitutions in America," in C. Peter Magrath, ed., *Constitutionalism and Politics: Conflict and Consensus* (Glenview, Ill.: Scott, Foresman, 1968), p. 30.

40. See analysis of the national infrastructure in Chapters 3 and 7.

3

The Constitutional Convention: The National Infrastructure

> By 1787 most statesmen were ready to accept what some twenty years before they had so bitterly resisted at the hands of Britain— a central government having the power to tax and to regulate commerce.
>
> Alfred H. Kelly and Winfred A. Harbison[1]

> Indeed, the principal weakness of the central government under the Articles of Confederation was its lack of power to levy taxes.
>
> A. T. Mason and William E. Beaney[2]

> The executive problem was thus primarily one of law enforcement, the institution of a department well enough equipped with power to see to it that the laws were faithfully executed in distant Georgia and individualistic western Pennsylvania and western Massachusetts as well as in the commercial centers of the seaboard.
>
> Charles C. Thach, Jr.[3]

The Constitutional Convention of 1787 had in effect two sessions,[4] one from May 29 to July 26, the other from August 6 to September 17.[5] Recognition of these two periods can help us distinguish between (a) the "Virginia Plan" discussed during the first session[6] and the "draft constitution" prepared during the interim recess[7] and considered during the second period;[8] and (b) the three-function infrastructure of the Virginia Plan and the high-policy superstructure of the draft constitution.[9]

One striking difference is the limited character of the "national executive" in the first session[10] and the broad, positive functions of the "president" in the second.[11] That contrast is important in this study of the separate group character of the houses of Congress and the president because the draft constitution gave the presidency elevated roles in the executive system and initiating rights and duties in the legislative system as well as a potential place in the representational process.[12]

This chapter will examine the Virginia Plan and the first period of the convention. The following chapter will consider the draft constitution and the second session of the convention.

NATIONAL INSTITUTIONS OF THE VIRGINIA PLAN

The set of resolutions introduced at the start of the Constitutional Convention reflects the large state nationalism of both Pennsylvania and Virginia. It is called the Virginia Plan because Governor Edmund Randolph of Virginia presented it on May 29, 1787.[13] Three functionally identified institutions were proposed: a legislature of two branches, an executive, and a judiciary. Its strongly national bent is evident from the principles stated the next day by Governor Randolph:

> 1. That a Union of the States merely federal will not accomplish the objects proposed by the Articles of Confederation, that is, common defence, security of liberty, and general welfare.
> 2. That no treaty or treaties among the whole or part of the states, as individual Sovereignties, would be sufficient.
> 3. That a *national* Government ought to be established consisting of a *supreme* Legislative, Executive and Judiciary.[14]

The term *federal* at that time probably meant what we now call *confederal* in full contrast to a unitary nation.[15] All three principles suggest a unitary national government and that the states might need to give up internal sovereignty.[16]

Some delegates were disturbed at these prospects.[17] The discussion that followed, according to *Madison's Notes*, focused upon the words *national* and *supreme*.[18] When Charles Pinckney (S.C.) asked Randolph "whether he meant to abolish the State Governments altogether," Randolph's reply was evasive. He said that these "general propositions" were "merely to introduce the particular ones which explained the outlines of the system he had in mind."[19]

The Virginia Plan proposed that the national legislature have power:

(1) to enjoy the Legislative Rights vested in the Congress by the Confederation and moreover

(2) to legislate in all cases to which the separate States are incompetent, or in which the harmony of the United States may be interrupted by the exercise of individual Legislation

(3) to negative all laws passed by the several states, contravening in the opinion of the National Legislature the articles of Union and

(4) to call forth the force of the Union against any member of the Union failing to fulfill its duty under the articles thereof.[20]

These additions to the powers of the Congress under the Confederation definitely concern the nation-state conflict, and proposals 2, 3, and 4 clearly indicate the supremacy of the national government.

The powers proposed for the national executive also are stated in general terms, and they suggest that executive power is subsequent and subordinate to legislative power: "besides a general authority to execute the National laws, it [the national executive] ought to enjoy the Executive rights vested in Congress by the Confederation."[21] The two powers of the national executive seem comparable, in reverse order, to the first two powers of the national legislature.

The antistate character of the Virginia Plan is evident from the third and fourth powers proposed. One allows the national legislature to negative state laws, and the other permits it to call forth "the force of the Union" against any defaulting state. The latter received so little support that it was dropped promptly.

The powers proposed for the national executive definitely associate it with the enforcement of national laws. Charles C. Thach's thorough analysis of the presidency in the convention says that "the original concept of executive power held by the Convention was that primarily of law enforcement."[22]

During the first two weeks, the delegates met as a "Committee of the Whole." This parliamentary device permitted flexible procedure for the revision of resolutions. The committee report of revised resolutions on June 13, 1787, filled out some details with respect to the national executive. That office was to be a single person, chosen by the national legislature, for a single term of seven years.[23]

THE CONFLICTS ON REPRESENTATION

The reactions of the Convention delegates were increasingly anti-national. The revised resolutions of June 13 allowed the state legislatures full choice on selection of members of the second branch of the national legislature. The antinational opposition took more concentrated form on June 15 when William Patterson of New Jersey presented a pro-state plan. Other states, such as Connecticut and Maryland, probably had a hand in the formulation of that plan. In general, it would be more amending of the Articles of Confederation than a new Constitution.[24] It proposed that the Congress of the Confederation be empowered to levy a tax on imports and to regulate commerce. This was the minimum authority if the central arrangement was to have sufficient internal sovereignty and enough infrastructure to function as a national government.

The New Jersey Plan also suggested a "federal Executive" of an unspecified number of persons. It suggested as well a provision declaring the supremacy of United States laws, along with a clause binding the judiciary of the states. This provision was largely accepted, as will be shown, by the convention in mid-July.

Beginning June 20 there were efforts to change *national* to *United States* in designating institutions.[25] The latter was more familiar and less objectionable. The Articles of Confederation had stated that the "stile" of the government was "The United States of America."

The controversy over representation in the branches of the national legislature led more and more to equality in the second branch. A motion on July 2 that each state should have one vote resulted in an even division of the states (Georgia itself being split). That and other matters were referred to a committee of 11 (1 from each state).

That special committee proposed a pattern of popular representation in the first branch, special powers in that branch on revenue measures, and one vote for each state in the second branch. This last was revised in the discussion to equality of vote for each state. The final package was approved five to four on July 16.[26] That arrangement of contrasting representation has been called the Great Compromise. It meant, among other things, that the high policy institutions would have the general form of the one, the few, and the many, like the classical mixed constitution.

The convention also accepted one proposition of the New Jersey Plan. This provided that the acts of Congress pursuant to the

Constitution are the supreme law of the states and that the judiciary of the several states shall be bound thereby. This came to the front when, on July 17, the convention voted six to three against the provision of the Virginia Plan authorizing the national legislature to negative laws deemed contrary to the "Articles of Union," as the new charter was then called.[27]

Immediately Luther Martin of Maryland moved for the supremacy clause of the New Jersey Plan, and it was approved without vote.[28] It became the second paragraph of Article VI of the final Constitution.

DIVERSE OPINIONS ON THE POWERS OF THE "NATIONAL EXECUTIVE"

The debates on the Virginia Plan during the first half of the Constitutional Convention provide us with a considerable range of beliefs about the "national executive." The plan itself said the executive was to be chosen by the national legislature, but it did not say whether the executive should be single or plural, and it left open the length of the term but denied eligibility for a second term.

With respect to the authority of the national executive, the Virginia Plan stated "that besides a general authority to execute the National laws, it ought to enjoy the Executive rights vested in Congress by the Confederation." When the proposal was discussed on June 1, Pinckney of South Carolina expressed fear that the "Executive Powers of the existing Congress might extend to peace and war, etc., which would render the Executive a monarchy, of the worst kind, to wit an elective one." The provision about the executive rights of the Confederation Congress was eliminated promptly.[29]

The comments of particular delegates covered a considerable range. The most restrictive concept reported in Madison's journal is that of Sherman of Connecticut:

> Mr. Sherman said he considered the Executive magistracy as nothing more than an institution for carrying the will of the Legislature into effect, that the person or persons ought to be appointed and accountable to the Legislature only, which was the depositary of the supreme will of the Society (June 1, 1787).[30]

The next day John Dickenson of Delaware expressed a quite different viewpoint. Madison's *Journal* reports these comments:

The Legislative, Executive, and Judiciary departments ought to be made as independent as possible; . . . a firm executive could only exist in a limited monarchy. . . . It was certain that equal blessings had never yet been derived from any of the republican form [sic]. A limited Monarchy however was out of the question (John Dickenson, June 2, 1787).[31]

We will see that later Alexander Hamilton and Gouveneur Morris expressed the need for an executive appointed for good behavior or for life. The more significant views would seem to be those of James Madison and James Wilson. On this matter, their ideas conformed to the convention position in the Virginia Plan—the executive is to keep order much more than to change it.

Madison in the discussion of June 1, 1787, suggested that the choice between unity and plurality might be affected by the extent of the executive authority. He moved that the national executive have power "to carry into effect the national Laws to appoint to offices in cases not otherwise provided for, and to execute such other powers 'not legislative nor judiciary in their nature,' as may from time to time be delegated by the national Legislature" (James Madison, June 1, 1787).[32] This shows that the initial approach to executive power focuses upon the enforcement of the national laws, the need for appointed officers in the operation, and the right and perhaps the duty of the national legislature to grant the executive additional powers.

Pinckney of South Carolina objected to the clause about other powers on the ground that it was unnecessary. With these words removed, Madison's motion carried.[33] Madison's journal reports somewhat similar views by James Wilson on the same day:

Mr. Wilson preferred a single magistrate, as giving most energy, dispatch and responsibility to the office. He did not consider the Prerogatives of the British Monarch as a proper guide in defining the Executive powers. Some of these prerogatives were of Legislative nature. Among others that of war and peace. The only powers he conceived strictly executive were those of executing the laws, and appointing officers, not appertaining to and appointed by the Legislature (James Wilson, June 1, 1787).[34]

Present-day advocates of a "strong presidency" are inclined to emphasize the first portion of the statement, on the "energy, dispatch and responsibility" of a single magistrate. But they tend to avoid the limited identification of powers in the last part of the statement.

However, the final action of the convention on the Virginia Plan, that is, the 23 resolutions adopted on July 26, 1787, and referred to the Committee of Detail for the drafting of a constitution, had that limited statement of the rights of the national executive. Resolution XII recognized "power to carry into execution the national laws" and to appoint to offices not otherwise provided for. Resolution XIII gave the executive veto of legislative actions.[35]

A few delegates favored a three-man executive, or perhaps a separate executive for each of three areas of the United States, such as south, middle, and north. Governor Randolph and George Mason of Virginia had views of this nature. This has caused some analysts to treat them as antinational. But Randolph appeared to be strongly antistate. On June 11 he made the following statement:

> The Executive and Judiciary of the States, notwithstanding their nominal independence of the State Legislatures, are in fact so dependent on them, that unless they be brought under some tie to the National System, they will always lean too much on the State systems, wherever a contest arises between the two (Governor Randolph, June 11, 1787).[36]

This indicates strongly that Randolph wished a national government that would be much less dependent upon state officials. Even a three-man national executive would be stronger than a 13-state executive. Moreover, Randolph and Mason may have thought that some concession to the three main areas of the country was necessary to assure ratification of the Constitution. Randolph and Mason tended to be cautious and may have feared rejection. But a three-man national executive would still have been stronger than a 13-state executive.

The most relevant fact about the early discussion of the power of the national executive may be the implicit emphasis upon the basic elements of government, that is, the authority to enforce taxes or regulations upon persons within the states. This is one main reason for the position here that the first half of the convention concerned the establishment of an infrastructure of internal sovereignty.

James Madison and James Wilson were the most active delegates, and their opposition to overactive state legislatures was a major factor in their support of strong national institutions. Madison, early in the convention, advocated the Virginia Plan proposal of a veto by the national legislature of state legislation. In the *Federalist*, he complained that the legislative department "was drawing all power in its impetuous vortex."[37]

Wilson favored popular election of the presidents. Some consider him democratic, but he disliked the democratic legislature in Pennsylvania.[38] Madison and Wilson sought a strong national executive as a check upon the legislature.[39] They repeatedly urged convention approval of the Council of Revision proposed in the Virginia Plan. The council would be the national executive and "a convenient number of the national Judiciary." Its dissent to a legislative bill meant rejection unless the legislature passed the act again.[40] Madison and Wilson sought a number of times to have the convention approve the Council of Revision (June 4, 6, July 21, August 15, 1787). They had only meager support each time.[41]

Their efforts here indicate that their interest in a strong president was in large measure for the negative purpose of checking the legislature. Also, the inclusion of judges in the council indicates that the executive was not as strong as they wished. The opponents of the council said that it would weaken the judiciary. Apparently this was a lesser matter for Madison and Wilson.

Presidentialists of this century, even those eager for welfare liberalism, make more of Alexander Hamilton than either Madison or Wilson. For instance, Professor James MacGregor Burns of Williams College in his 1973 book *Presidential Government,* asserts that "the modern theory of presidential power" is "the contribution primarily of Alexander Hamilton."[42] Hamilton's record as the first secretary of the treasury in leading congressional approval of financial legislation seems to be a better basis for Burns's evaluation than Hamilton's actions at the convention or during the ratification.

Hamilton presented a comprehensive plan of government in a five-hour speech on June 18, 1787 at the Constitutional Convention. The national "governor" and senators would serve for "good behavior," that is, for life. The states would be mere administrative units.[43] The delegates gave the plan little if any support.

In the *Federalist*, Hamilton explained that the presidency would be less powerful in several ways than the British king and, in a few ways, than the governor of New York.[44] He also said that treaty-making power is neither legislative nor executive but "a distinct department."[45] In the New York ratification debate, he said that the legislature has three branches and the executive two branches.[46] In a 1793 newspaper debate with Madison, Hamilton treated government as having only legislative, executive, and judicial departments.[47] In that dispute he denied Congress authority with respect to a proclamation of neutrality.[48]

THE LEGISLATIVE AND EXECUTIVE POWERS
AT MIDCONVENTION

On July 26, 1787, the Constitutional Convention completed eight weeks of discussion on the Virginia Plan. The original resolutions had been expanded and altered, and on that day the convention referred 23 approved resolutions to a five-member Committee of Detail for the drafting of a constitution.

We are particularly concerned with the determination at that time of the legislative and executive powers. It may be helpful to compare the final position of the first half of the convention with the beginning position of the second half, as set forth in the draft constitution reported on August 6, 1787. Accordingly, the resolutions adopted July 26, 1787, concerning the legislative and executive powers of the national government, are presented below.

Both types of powers were stated in broad terms. Those of the national legislature were stated in one paragraph:

> VI. RESOLVED. That the national legislature ought to possess the legislative rights vested in Congress by the confederation, and moreover, to legislate in all cases for the general interests of the union, and also in those to which the states are separately incompetent, or in which the harmony of the United States may be interrupted by the exercise of individual legislation.[49]

Thus the scope of the national legislative power at that point was described quite broadly but with much emphasis upon the inadequacy of individual state legislation.

The powers of the national executive at midconvention were also stated simply but more precisely. They were in two resolutions:

> XII. RESOLVED. That a national executive be instituted, to consist of a single person; to be chosen by the national legislature, for the term of seven years; to be ineligible a second time; with power to carry into execution the national laws; to appoint to offices not otherwise provided for; to be removable on impeachment, and conviction of malpractice or neglect of duty; to receive a fixed compensation for the devotion of his time to publick service; to be paid out of the publick treasury.
>
> XIII. RESOLVED. That the national executive shall have a right to negative any legislative act, which shall not be afterwards passed, unless by two third parts of each branch of the national legislature.[50]

Thus the national executive at midconvention was concerned with the application of acts of the national legislative. The group character of the national institutions concerned enforcement of duties. We will see that the draft constitution that was reported ten days later introduced the concepts of Congress and president and gave them a positive group character based upon what is necessary and proper for the national system.

NOTES

1. Alfred Kelly and Winfred Harbison, *The American Constitution: Its Origins and Development*, 4th ed. (New York: Norton, 1970), p. 114.
2. A. T. Mason and William E. Beaney, *American Constitutional Law*, 5th ed. (Englewood Cliffs, N.J.: Prentice-Hall, 1972), p. 263.
3. Charles C. Thach, Jr., *The Creation of the Presidency* (Baltimore: Johns Hopkins University Press, 1922), p. 77.
4. Most analysts do not point out the difference between the two periods. See, for example, Arthur N. Holcombe, *The Constitutional System* (Chicago: Scott, Foresman, 1964), pp. 39–86; David G. Smith, *The Convention and the Constitution* (New York: St. Martin's Press, 1965); Alpheus T. Mason, *Free Government in the Making* (New York: Oxford University Press, 1965); Andrew C. McLaughlin, *A Constitutional History of the United States* (New York: Appleton-Century-Crofts, 1935), pp. 148–97; Edward S. Corwin, *The Constitution and what it means today* (Princeton: Princeton University Press, 1958).
5. Winton U. Solberg, ed., *The Federal Convention and the Formation of the Union of the American States* (Indianapolis: Bobbs-Merrill, 1958), pp. 73, 249–58, 339.
6. Ibid., pp. 73–130.
7. Ibid., pp. 246–69.
8. Ibid., pp. 269–339. There is a limited analysis of the work of the Committee of Detail in Max Farrand, *The Framing of the Constitution of the United States* (New Haven: Yale University Press, 1913), pp. 124–59. See also Max Farrand, *The Records of the Federal Convention of 1787*, vol. 2 (New Haven: Yale University Press, 1911), pp. 129–75, for "a number of documents evidently relating to the work of the Committee of Detail." These were found among the Wilson Papers in the Library of the Historical Society of Pennsylvania. They seem to raise more questions than they answer.
9. See Chapter 13.
10. See the section entitled "Functional Interdependence of Criminal Law Processes" in Chapter 2.
11. Solberg, *Federal Convention*, pp. 265–66.
12. See Chapters 1, 4, and 14.
13. Solberg, *Federal Convention*, p. 73.
14. Ibid., pp. 80–81.
15. Gouveneur Morris asserted on May 30, 1787, that there can be only one supreme power in a community. Alexander Hamilton on June 18 said "Two

sovereignties cannot coexist within the same limits." Solberg, *Federal Convention*, pp. 81, 144.

16. See the section entitled "Need for Partial Nationalization of Internal Sovereignty" in Chapter 2.

17. Solberg, *Federal Convention*, p. 81; see also *Notes of Debates in the Federal Convention of 1787 Reported by James Madison* (New York: Norton, 1966), p. 34 (hereafter cited as *Madison's Notes*).

18. Ibid.

19. Solberg, *Federal Convention*, p. 81.

20. *Madison's Notes*, p. 31.

21. Ibid.

22. Charles C. Thach, Jr., *The Creation of the Presidency: 1775-1789: A Study in Constitutional History* (Baltimore: Johns Hopkins University Press, 1923, p. 119; "To take the Constitution from its historical setting is to fail to comprehend its meaning or that of its separate parts." Ibid., p. 22.

23. Solberg, *Federal Convention*, pp. 127-30.

24. Ibid., pp. 131-34.

25. The revised resolutions of June 13 used the term *national* 26 times, while the resolutions adopted on July 26 used it only 13 times. See, in general, Farrand, *Framing of the Constitution*, pp. 91-112.

26. Solberg, *Federal Convention*, p. 222.

27. *Madison's Notes*, p. 305.

28. Ibid., p. 306.

29. Ibid., pp. 45, 48.

30. Ibid., p. 46.

31. Ibid., pp. 56-57.

32. Ibid., p. 47.

33. Ibid., pp. 47-48.

34. Ibid., p. 46.

35. Ibid., p. 383; Solberg, *Federal Convention*, p. 255.

36. *Madison's Notes*, p. 105.

37. *The Federalist Papers—Hamilton—Madison—Jay* (New York: New American Library, 1961), p. 309.

38. Charles Page Smith, *James Wilson: Founding Father, 1742-1798* (Chapel Hill: University of North Carolina Press, 1956), pp. 100, 107-109.

39. *Madison's Notes*, p. 88.

40. Solberg, *Federal Convention*, p. 78.

41. *Madison's Notes*, pp. 66-67, 79-80, 336-43.

42. James MacGregor Burns, *Presidential Government*. Sentry edition (Boston: Houghton Mifflin, 1973), p. 17. One analysis, however, questions the relevance of Hamilton's view to the contemporary scene: Alpheus T. Mason and Richard H. Leach, *In Quest of Freedom: American Political Thought and Practice* (Englewood Cliffs, N.J.: Prentice-Hall, 1959), p. 180.

43. *Madison's Notes*, pp. 129-39.

44. *The Federalist Papers*, pp. 449-64.

45. Ibid., p. 450-51.

46. Jonathan Elliot, *The Debates in the Several State Conventions*, vol. 2 (Philadelphia: J. B. Lippincott, 1961), p. 348.

47. John C. Hamilton, ed., *The Works of Alexander Hamilton*, vol. 2 (New York: John F. Trow, Printer, 1851), pp. 76–85; Robert S. Hirschfield, *The Power of the Presidency: Concepts and Controversy*, 3d ed. (Hawthorne, N.Y.: Aldine, 1982), pp. 59–65.

48. Hamilton seems to make a general rule out of the possibility of exceptional situations. "Wise politicians will be cautious about fettering the government with restrictions that cannot be observed, because they know that every breach of the fundamental laws, though dictated by necessity, impairs that sacred reverence which ought to be maintained in the breast of rulers towards the constitution of a country, and forms a precedent for other breaches where the same plea of necessity does not exist at all, or is less urgent and palpable." *The Federalist Papers*, no. 25, p. 167. Hamilton seems to oppose limitations because of the possibility of exceptions and the inability to differentiate among exceptions. The exceptions made during the Civil War did not result in extermination of limitations. Hamilton's apparent inability to deal with exceptions as exceptions may be found among contemporary analysts.

49. *Madison's Notes*, pp. 380–83; Solberg, *Federal Convention*, pp. 252–55.

50. Solberg, *Federal Convention*, pp. 252–55.

4

The Constitutional Convention: The Tripartite Superstructure

For all practical purposes, it is irrelevant to argue whether a particular power has been given to Congress or to the President. Each branch recognizes its dependence on the other and usually foregoes action unless it has at least the tacit consent of the other branch.

Philippa Strum[1]

The framers purposely split the military power of the United States between Congress and the president. Neither could control the military apparatus without the other.

James P. Pfiffner[2]

The most practical method of unifying people is to give them a symbol with which all can identify. If the symbol is human, its efficacy is enhanced enormously. . . . the founding fathers established the presidency as a position of reverence.

George Reedy[3]

The midconvention draft constitution of the Committee of Detail went above and beyond the resolutions of the Virginia Plan that the convention had referred to the committee. It broadened and elevated the dimensions of the Constitution in several ways:

First, it enlarged the legal and spiritual scope of the Constitution and thus permitted the development of the three-power representational group and the public policy superstructure.[4]

Second, it particularized the legislative powers and thus avoided the implication of unlimited national power. At the same time it related national power, not to the incompetence and disharmony of the states, but to what is necessary and proper for the national society.

Third, it considered treaty making to be a distinct type of power separate from legislation, execution, and judicial action.

Fourth, it elevated the role of the president with respect to the execution of laws and assigned that office positive duties in the legislative process.

This chapter will discuss the expanded scope of the draft constitution of August 6. Particular provisions relating to Congress and the presidency will be discussed in Chapters 5, 6, 10, and 11.

THE CHARACTER OF THE COMMITTEE OF DETAIL

On July 24, 1787, the Constitutional Convention selected "a Committee to report a Constitution conformable to the Resolutions passed by the Convention."[5] This was in the eighth week of the convention, and during that period the delegates had discussed, debated, and in key ways revised the resolutions of the Virginia Plan. The plan had been presented at the start of the "main business" of the convention on May 29, 1787. Now the convention was calling for a draft constitution, which would be the basis of the discussions and debates for the remainder of the convention. There was a ten-day recess from July 26 to August 6, when the committee reported its draft constitution. Consideration of it continued until the end of the convention on September 17, 1787.

The five members of what was called the Committee of Detail were chosen by ballot. The delegates selected were John Rutlidge, chairman, South Carolina; Governor Edmund Randolph, Virginia; Nathaniel Gorham, Massachusetts; Oliver Ellsworth, Connecticut; and James Wilson, Pennsylvania. James Madison and Alexander Hamilton, who were to be the main authors of the *Federalist Papers,* defending the Constitution for ratification purposes, were not elected members of the committee that drafted the constitution for the last half of the convention.

We will see that the contribution of that committee was much more than matters of detail.[6] It made the Constitution more acceptable, more positive, and more open to expansion and elevation. If there are unsung heroes of the convention, they are the more moderate members of that committee: Rutlidge, Gorham, and Ellsworth.

The committee accomplished much during the ten-day recess, and its report was largely approved. Its success may have been due to its small size—only five members—and to its balance. We will see that it contained one nationalist and four moderates.[7]

The geographical distribution was favorable to acceptance of its report. The five states were spread north, central, and south. Each of the members was from the tidewater aristocracy rather than the commonalty of the hinterland, but that was true of most of the delegates at the convention. Both the agricultural and the commercial states were represented. Two of the members were from slave states, but slavery was not yet the national moral issue that it later became.[8]

The population rank of the five states was Virginia (1), Pennsylvania (2), Massachusetts (3), Connecticut (6), and South Carolina (8). Gorham, Ellsworth, and Rutlidge had favored equality of states in the second branch of the national legislature.

The legislative disposition of the five members, individually and collectively, is more important than their geographical distribution. On the general nation/state conflict, Wilson was a strong nationalist, while the others were more or less in the middle.[9] They were partly national and partly confederal. Later, that mixture was called *federal,* but at the start of the convention that term still meant what we now call *confederal.* The new meaning of *federal* became more apparent in the ratification period, but the underlying idea began to develop at the convention among the more moderate and pragmatic delegates.

All five members of the Committee of Detail were comparatively active throughout the convention. On May 25, when business could begin, Rutlidge, Randolph, and Wilson were present. Rutlidge seconded the motion that General Washington preside at the convention. Gorham and Ellsworth arrived on May 28.

Randolph was the primary actor. He began the "main business" on May 29 with a daylong presentation of the Virginia Plan. On the next day, the convention went into the procedural status of a Committee of the Whole. This allowed freer discussion and less rigid methods than formal parliamentary status. Gorham, a future member of the Committee of Detail, was elected by ballot to preside. During the preceding year, he had been the president of the Confederation Congress. For the first two weeks of the convention, he, rather than

Washington, presided over the proceedings. On June 13 he reported 19 approved resolutions to the convention proper. These revised in part the 15 resolutions of the original Virginia Plan. The convention considered those 19 resolutions until further revised resolutions for the drafting of a constitution were referred to the Committee of Detail on July 26.

This means that Gorham could bring much knowledge and legislative leadership to the Committee of Detail. It also shows that Gorham was known and respected by many delegates. Many of them had served in the predecessor Congress. Gorham had long legislative experience in his own state, having been three times Speaker of its House. He was, incidentally, the only member of the Committee of Detail who was not a lawyer.

James Wilson had the most brilliant mind of the committee members and perhaps of all convention delegates. He had been born in Scotland and had studied philosophy at St. Andrews University.[10] After settling in Philadelphia, he studied law with John Dickenson, later the principal author of the Articles of Confederation and also a delegate at the 1787 Convention. Wilson served in the Continental Congress and signed the Declaration of Independence. He was in the national administration during the war. His legal opinion that the Congress could charter an exclusive bank for North America set forth a theory of general powers that rivals that of Hamilton with respect to the Bank of the United States.[11]

Wilson was as active as Madison at the convention. They had much in common, both having a strong dislike of state legislatures and both advocating that the Council of Revision be composed of judges and the executive for the review of national legislation. They tried four times to obtain convention passage, but no more than three states supported them.[12] Wilson had drafting skill and probably had much to do with finishing the draft constitution.[13]

John Rutlidge was a southern aristocrat who owned a number of plantations in South Carolina. He was a London-trained lawyer, helped write the South Carolina constitution, and served in the Stamp Act Congress and the First and Second Continental Congresses. He was active at the 1787 convention from the start. Madison's *Notes* show that Rutlidge participated in the debate ten times during the first two weeks. He was also moderately active in the month-long debate on the modes of representation in the two branches of the national legislature.[14]

Rutlidge early sought specification in the powers granted the national legislature[15] but the Virginia Plan prevailed at that time.[16] Rutlidge complained that "incompetence" of the states was too vague a standard for Congressional power.

The draft constitution of the Committee of Detail eliminated the state incompetency clause and particularized the powers of Congress. Thus Rutlidge finally gained his point and convinced others of the need for enumeration. There is also the fact that such an attitude may have been known to the delegates when they chose Rutlidge on July 26. Thus there was to some degree an authorization by the convention for matters that committee members had asserted prior to their selection.

Rutlidge, Wilson, and Randolph, three future members of the Committee of Detail, expressed views on the national executive during the June 1 session. The first two favored a single executive, but Randolph favored a three-man executive. Two days later, he explained that the three should be drawn from different areas of the country.[17]

Rutlidge put forward a number of positions that met with limited success. He advocated that the first branch of the legislature be elected by the state legislatures (June 6); that the states be divided into three classes, with one, two, or three members in the legislature (June 8); that the suffrage in the first branch be proportioned to "the quota of contribution" (June 11); that the representatives have two-year terms, rather than one-year, as proposed by Ellsworth (June 12); and that the members of the second branch receive no salary (June 12). Rutlidge and Wilson came into conflict on June 21 when the former favored election of representatives by the state legislatures and the latter by the people directly (June 21).

For about a month, beginning June 20. 1787, there was general debate or discussion on the modes of representation in the two branches of the national legislature. Many delegates participated, including all five future members of the Committee of Detail. The large states tended to be nationalistic and favored representation proportionate to population or wealth. The smaller states tended to be "federal," that is, confederal, and favored equality of the states as in the Confederation Congress. Bicameralism provided means for compromise with different modes for the two houses. Some smaller states sought a proportionate method that did not give full force to population or wealth.[18]

The other two future members of the Committee of Detail, Ellsworth of Connecticut and Gorham of Massachusetts, seem to have started a process that helped the Great Compromise with their motion of June 20, 1787. This involved a choice of terms, but it enhanced the "federal" cause. They moved and seconded that the introductory resolution for a "National Government of a supreme legislative, executive, and judiciary" be changed to a "Government of the United States" of three such powers. The official name of the confederation was "The United States of America." Their motion eliminated the use of "national" in favor of the more familiar and more acceptable name "United States." That had sufficient ambiguity or flexibility to stand for a confederal, a federal, and a national system. But its immediate use at the time probably was antinational.

We will see that the draft constitution reported by the Committee of Detail on August 6 eliminated all use of the word *national*. It used the term *United States* even in dealing with particular institutions. Moreover, it introduced such proper names as *Congress* and *president*. They, too, were being used in the Articles of Confederation and thus were more familiar, less ominous, and more widely acceptable than such stark terms as *national legislative* and *national executive*. [19]

During the month before the election of the Committee of Detail, the convention debated the composition of the legislative branches. Madison and Wilson favored popular representation and hence the dominance of the large states. Ellsworth argued that the small states need protection from the large ones. He stressed that the situation of the country was marked by mixture and compromise and that there should be equality of states in the second branch. Gorham and Rutlidge tended to favor that position. The attitudes of these three lesser-known delegates may help to explain their election to the committee to draft a constitution.

EXPANDED PATTERN OF THE DRAFT CONSTITUTION

The Committee of Detail supplied much more than details when transforming the revised resolutions of the Virginia Plan into a draft constitution. It gave the Constitution much more positive capacity for adaptation, expansion, and elevation.

The Virginia Plan had called for a national legislature of two branches, a national executive, and a national judiciary. The committee eliminated all uses of *national* and introduced the terms *Congress, House of Representatives, Senate,* and *president,* as well as *the United States.*

The committee surmounted the enforcement sequence of legislative, executive, and judicial functions, with the institutionally separated trio of House, Senate, and president, and their shared responsibilities with respect to representation, communication, and the integration of conflicts. These changes enhanced the acceptability of taxation and regulation and allowed the House, the Senate, and the president to have functions beyond legislative and executive ones.[20]

The draft constitution had 23 articles, but there was little similarity between the corresponding numbers of the articles and the 23 resolutions referred to the committee.

The draft constitution began with a Preamble and two introductory articles. The Preamble, which was entirely new, declared that "the people . . . do ordain, declare and establish the following Constitution." But unlike the final Constitution, the founders were not "the People of the United States," but rather the people of 13 named states.[21] That might mean 13 bodies of people to those who were prostate, or one body of people to those who were pronational, and perhaps something else to those who were pragmatic moderates. In any event, the Preamble seems to be a good example of the ways in which the Committee of Detail made the Constitution more acceptable to the several state legislatures or the other bodies of persons who might act upon the ratification of the Constitution.

The Preamble may have a somewhat hidden meaning or intention. It may have been designed to suggest that the authority of the national government does not come from the state legislatures but from the people of the several states. The convention, on July 23, which was close to the time of authorizing the Committee of Detail, discussed the means of approval or ratification. Wilson and others had opposed the presentation of the Constitution to the state legislatures. Hence, the draft constitution may have been laying the foundation for submission to state conventions of representatives of the voters of the several states.

Article I of the draft constitution gave the government the same name as that prescribed in the Articles of Confederation, that is, "The United States of America."[22] This could serve both the pro-state and the pronational forces depending upon whether the emphasis is placed upon "United" or "States."

Article II of the draft constitution provided that "The Government shall consist of supreme legislative, executive and judicial powers."[23] The comparable statement in the Virginia Plan had not used the term *powers* and may have meant institutions rather than functions. But Article II was omitted from the final constitution.

The most incisive provisions in the draft constitution are probably the initial sentences of the articles dealing with Congress, the Senate, the president, and the Supreme Court, that is, Articles III, IX, X, and XI:

[III] The legislative power shall be vested in a Congress, to consist of two separate and distinct bodies of men, a House of Representatives and a Senate; each of which shall in all cases have a negative on the other.

[IX] The Senate of the United States shall have the power to make treaties and to appoint ambassadors, and judges of the Supreme Court.

[X] The Executive Power of the United States shall be vested in a single person. His stile shall be, "The President of the United States of America;" and his title shall be, "His Excellency."

[XI] The Judicial Power of the United States shall be vested in one Supreme Court, and in such inferior Courts as shall, when necessary, from time to time, be constituted by the Legislature of the United States.[24]

These Provisions do not limit the institutions to a single function, such as legislation for Congress and execution for the president. Other provisions may restrict the courts to cases or controversies, but Congress and the president may each have two or more functions (see Chapters 5 and 6). The quoted provisions also indicate that the Senate, and perhaps other institutions, may have functions that are not legislative, executive, or judicial.

Seven articles (III–IX) dealt with the houses of Congress. Article III provided that the "legislative power shall be vested in a Congress, to consist of two separate and distinct bodies of men, a House of Representatives, and a Senate." Each house is to have a negative on the other. The legislature is to meet the first Monday in December every year. This resulted in a newly elected Congress not meeting until a year later, but that was remedied by the Twentieth Amendment in 1933.

Articles IV and V dealt with the election and orgnanization of the House of Representatives and the Senate, respectively. The draft constitution added many important details. Article VI gave the state legislators initial authority to hold the elections of representatives. It also dealt with legislative procedure, and the final section elaborated the executive veto power stipulated in Resolution XIII, which had been referred to the Committee of Detail ten days before.

A number of the other articles of the draft constitution will be examined in the remaining sections of this chapter. Article VII, which particularizes the legislative power, and Article VIII, which declares the supremacy of national laws, will be considered in the next section, "Eighteen Legislative Powers and One Executive Power."

EIGHTEEN LEGISLATIVE POWERS AND ONE EXECUTIVE POWER

The Committee of Detail transformed the foremost general power into numerous specific powers. The actions of the convention that were referred to the committee on July 26, 1787, included a single resolution with respect to legislative authority. This gave the national legislature the right "to legislate in all cases for the general interests of the union, and also in those to which the states are separately incompetent, or in which the harmony of the United States may be interrupted by the exercise of individual legislation."[25]

The action of the committee in replacing this with 18 particular grants reflects the objection asserted on the third day of the convention, May 31, 1787, by one of the future members of the Committee of Detail, John Rutlidge. He and his fellow delegate from South Carolina, Charles Pinckney, objected to the vagueness of the term *incompetent.* They stated that "they could not well decide how to vote until they should see an exact enumeration of the powers comprehended by this definition."[26]

At that time, Governor Randolph defended the provision of the Virginia Plan by disclaiming any intention to give indefinite power to the national legislature. Madison added a stronger defense. He asserted that he was strongly opposed to "enumeration and definition of the powers necessary to be exercised by the national legislature." The convention then approved the Virginia Plan in this regard. That part of the plan remained and was included in the July 26 resolutions that were referred to the Committee of Detail for the draft of a constitution.[27] But the final Constitution, as will be shown, does enumerate the powers of Congress, despite the opposition of Madison.

When the committee met during the recess, John Rutlidge apparently still had his objection to the general authorization. Some other committee members also had doubts. In any event, the report of the committee included an enumeration of the legislative powers of Congress. It specified 18 particular grants. The format remained intact. Two of the 18 were replaced, but the final Constitution also includes an enumeration of 18 legislative powers. The first is the power to impose and collect taxes. The last is the power of Congress to enact all laws "necessary and proper" to carry into execution the powers of the governments and its departments and officers.[28]

The contrast between the first and the last reflects the demands by Ellsworth on June 29 for a strong basis of legislative, executive, and judicial powers coupled with the recognition of future necessities.[29]

The particularization of the legislative powers of Congress resulted in a language adjustment by the Committee of Style in the final days of the convention. The provision that "legislative power" shall be vested in Congress was changed to the "legislative powers herein granted" shall be vested in Congress.[30] This probably was an assurance to the pro-state delegations that Congress would not have general legislative authority and thus further reduce the power of the states.

That limitation on legislative power also would be a limitation upon "executive power," if that means the authority to execute the laws enacted by Congress. Such a meaning appears in the resolution on the rights of the national executive sent to the Committee of Detail on July 26, 1787. That "executive power" may be singular and general and thus applies to all 18 or more types of legislation.

The different manner in which the draft constitution presented the legislative and executive powers should be emphasized. It specified numerous areas of legislative power, such as the power to tax, the power to regulate commerce, and the power to punish counterfeit. But it prescribed only one "executive power"; it did not specify a power to execute tax laws, another power to execute laws of regulation, and still another to execute laws against counterfeiting. That would seem to explain why "executive power" was left singular whereas "legislative power" was made plural.

The "executive power" is singular and general; it is power to execute any of the 18 or more types of legislation by Congress. It is similar to the power of the "national executive" in Resolution XII, which was approved July 26 and referred to the committee.[31]

This interpretation agrees with the rule of construction that particular words are to be interpreted in light of the words with which they are associated. In the draft and final constitutions, "executive power" is between legislative power and judicial power. Similarly, presidential executive power is a function between congressional legislative power and the judicial power of the courts. This is a limited power and to a large extent executive power is now performed by subordinates. The president is concerned largely with other types of action.[32]

DOUBLE EMERGENCE OF THE PRESIDENCY

The draft constitution of August 6, 1787, introduced for the first time the office and title of the president. This was related, of course, to the elimination of the term *national* in relation to the executive or other institutions and the use of proper names such as United States, Congress, House of Representatives, Senate, and president.

The term *president* was in some use at the time. Three states used that title in place of *governor* for the chief executive position.[33] It also was the title of the presiding officer of the Congress of the Confederation. That officer was first among equals as is the present chairman of a board of directors rather than the first executive of a corporation. The use of the term *president* in the draft constitution for the primary executive position required, under the circumstances, some identifying explanation. The provision vesting the executive power of the United States in the president served that purpose and perhaps more.

The draft constitution dealt with the president in three major places: Article VI, Section 13; Article X, Section 1; and Article X, Section 2. The first of these concerned the veto power of the president. This provision in the draft constitution is essentially the same as that set forth in Resolution XIII in the list of convention adoptions referred to the Committee of Detail on July 26 for the drafting of a constitution.[34]

Section 1 of Article X of the draft constitution provided that "the Executive power of the United States shall be vested in a single person" to be called "the President of the United States of America." There is no explicit definition of "the Executive Power of the United States," but the convention delegates appear to have assumed that it has the same meaning as "the rights" of the "national executive" in the resolutions referred to the Committee of Detail on July 26.

Resolution XII of that group stated that the national executive has "power to carry into execution the national laws" and "to appoint to offices not otherwise provided for."[35]

That conclusion is fortified by the aforementioned rule of construction that words should be interpreted in light of their associated words.[36] Executive power thus applies the statutory enactments of Congress and may be subject to adjudication by the courts.

The sequence of statutory legislation, execution, and adjudication is the established order of functions in Anglo-U.S. criminal law process.

There is a *second* emergence of the president in Article X, Section 2, of the draft constitution and Article II, Sections 2 and 3, of the final Constitution. The content of these two is similar. Each prescribes several rights and duties for the president. They are not designated to be "executive powers." They are assigned directly and specifically to the president. They include roles that are close to the legislative process, the political administrative process, the judicial process, and the foreign/security process. For a single designation, *presidential* is much more appropriate than *executive.* Moreover, most of them do not fit in the position of being after congressional legislative functions and before the judicial functions of the courts. Some of the duties are prior to congressional legislative action. These include the duty to inform Congress on the state of the Union and the obligation to recommend measures that the president deems necessary and expedient.

Most of these specific rights and duties seem to elevate the president above the "infrastructure" function of execution and to high-level responsibilities that are more appropriate to a "superstructure." The clearest contrast of the two levels is in the difference between the provision vesting the executive power in the president and the subsequent provision obligating the president to take care that the laws be faithfully executed. The latter statement implies that other persons will do the executing, and it likewise suggests that the president will give guidance and scrutiny of others to the end that the laws are faithfully executed. The constitutional background of that provision in the state constitutions and in the landmark actions of Parliament indicates that the laws in question are those enacted by the representative legislatures.

NOTES

1. Philippa Strum, *Presidential Power and American Democracy* (Pacific Palisades, Calif.: Goodyear, 1979), p. 13.

2. James P. Pfiffner, *The President, the Budget, and Congress* (Boulder, Colo.: Westview Press, 1979), p. 70.

3. George Reedy, *The Twilight of the Presidency* (New York: New American Library, 1970), p. 21.

4. For brief descriptions of the three-power representational branch, sometimes called the public policy superstructure, see Chapters 1 and 13.

5. *Notes of Debates in the Federal Convention of 1787 Reported by James Madison* (New York: Norton, 1966), p. 362 (hereafter cited as *Madison's Notes*).

6. There is a limited analysis of the work of the Committee of Detail in Max Farrand, *The Framing of the Constitution of the United States* (New Haven: Yale University Press, 1913), p. 124. See Chapter 3, note 8.

7. The four "moderates" were Rutledge, Randolph, Gorham, and Ellsworth. In some respects Randolph was a large state nationalist. He proposed a three-man executive with one from each region, but he deplored the dependence of the state governors. See *Madison's Notes*, p. 105. On July 16 Randolph stated, "The vote of this morning [for equality of suffrage in the second branch] had embarrassed the business extremely." Ibid., p. 299.

8. "There was no sharp division here between slave and free states." Farrand, *Framing of the Constitution,* pp. 103, 110.

9. For biographical sketches of the delegates, see Winton U. Solberg, *The Federal Convention and the Formation of the Union* (Indianapolis: Bobbs-Merrill, 1953), pp. 387-405.

10. Charles P. Smith, *James Wilson: Founding Father, 1742-1798* (Chapel Hill: University of North Carolina Press, 1956), pp. 12-26.

11. Ibid., pp. 145-58. Randolph G. Adams, ed., *Selected Political Essays of James Wilson* (New York: Knopf, 1930), pp. 125-49.

12. *Madison's Notes* (June 4, 6, July 21, August 15), pp. 66, 81, 336, 461.

13. Farrand, *Framing of the Constitution*, pp. 125-26.

14. *Madison's Notes* (June 21, 23, 27, July 6, 10, 11, 16), pp. 167, 177, 201, 245, 260, 264, 270, 299, 300.

15. Ibid., p. 31.

16. Ibid., pp. 43-44.

17. Ibid., pp. 46, 58.

18. Ibid., pp. 95, 98, 103.

19. Solberg, *Federal Convention*, pp. 42–44, 258–69.

20. See the section entitled "Double Emergence of the Presidency" in this chapter.

21. *Madison's Notes*, p. 385.

22. Ibid.

23. Ibid.

24. Ibid., pp. 385–86, 391–93.

25. Ibid., p. 380.

26. Ibid., p. 43.

27. Ibid., pp. 44, 380.

28. Ibid., pp. 389–90, 620–21.

29. Ibid., p. 219.

30. Ibid., pp. 616, 622.

31. Ibid., p. 383.

32. See Chapters 6, 9, and 11.

33. Delaware, New Hampshire, and Pennsylvania used the title of president rather than governor. In Pennsylvania the president was in effect the chairman of an executive council of 12 elected officials.

34. *Madison's Notes*, p. 383.

35. Ibid.

36. There is a rule of construction *noscitur a sociis* that holds that "the meaning of a doubtful word may be ascertained by reference to the meaning of words associated with it." *Corpus Juris Secundum,* vol. 66, p. 607. Both the convention and the Constitution definitely associate "executive power" with "legislative power" and "judicial power," or comparable terms. Executive power is repeatedly placed between legislative and judicial power. Its place in that sequence is a strong indication of its meaning.

5

Congress in the Constitution

> . . . the architects of the Grand Design of 1787, keenly conscious of the incompetence of Congress under the confederation, expressly vested the primary powers of the new national and federal government in the Congress of the United States. From the place of prominence they give it in the fundamental framework and the vast powers they conferred upon it, the framers evidently intended to make Congress the central department in the new republic.
>
> George B. Galloway[1]

> The American presidency was not designed to be the center of leadership in the new republic. If any branch of government was to serve as a positive and innovative force in a system of carefully intermingled powers, it was the legislature.
>
> James MacGregor Burns[2]

> In republican government, the legislative authority necessarily predominates.
>
> James Madison[3]

The task of explaining the separate group purpose of the three elected institutions, as well as the larger problem of suggesting how the politically separated houses of Congress and the presidency can attain that goal is made considerably more difficult by particular aspects of the Constitutional Convention.

First, the Virginia Plan identified institutions by their functions and apparently assumed that each institution had only one function. There was no mention of the function of representation even though the legislative institution was constituted to be representational as well as legislative.

Second, when the Virginia Plan was replaced by the draft constitution, the representational-legislative institution was designated *Congress*. Article I of the final Constitution at first equates Congress and legislative power and then is quite detailed about some matters and rather vague about others.

This chapter will explain the constitutional provisions with respect to Congress. The application of the various powers will be discussed in Chapter 7, which will include the congressional establishment of the executive and judicial systems.

DOUBLE PRIMACY OF CONGRESS

Congress comes first in the Constitution because it is both representational and legislative. Article I takes up more than half the space of the Constitution and still does not tell all about certain aspects of its two houses and their functions.

The House of Representatives is directly representational. Its members are allocated by states with substantial consideration of the respective populations. The electors in each state must be qualified to vote for the most numerous branch of the state legislature. The Constitution does not explain the representational function, but it might be included in the "legislative process."[4]

After Article I explains the allocation of the members, it stipulates organizational details and then prescribes the law-making process including a presidential veto. Next, it particularizes powers and limitations. There are 18 specified areas of congressional authority and numerous limitations upon the national and state legislatures. The positive, initiating roles of the president are set forth in Article II.[5]

Article I is not the whole story of the powers of Congress. There are authorizations of one kind or another in later articles, as will be shown.[6] Yet there are several areas about which little is said. The authority of Congress over the executive system is based considerably upon implication and the general power to enact "necessary and proper" laws. Also, the authority to investigate official and unofficial developments has had to be inferred.[7]

As a general rule, modern constitutional republics have two pre-eminent elements. One is a mixed legislative process that includes an elected assembly, and the other is the rule of positive or statutory law.[8] The Constitution of 1787 combined these two in the House of Representatives, and now they are found in all three of the elected institutions.

There is a double primacy in this public policy superstructure, as we noted in the introduction to this book, because these institutions comprise both the legislative and the representational branches. At the Constitutional Convention if there were an order of priority in the three elements, the House was first, the Senate next, and then the president. Later chapters will examine whether this order has changed during the 200 years of our constitutional system.[9]

The convention clearly favored the primacy of written law. The second paragraph of Article VI reads:

> This Constitution, and the Laws of the United States which shall be made in Pursuance thereof, and all Treaties made, or which shall be made, under the Authority of the United States, shall be the supreme Law of the Land; and the Judges in every State shall be bound thereby, any Thing in the Constitution of Laws of any State, to the Contrary notwithstanding.

This provision clearly makes the laws and treaties of the United States, as well as its Constitution, superior to the constitutions and laws of the states.[10] It also suggests that the judiciary and not the legislative institution is to determine whether there is a conflict. The provision refers to judges of the states. It is obvious that the national judges would be bound by this supremacy clause. However, it will be shown that some state judges believed that they were to make the decision. The issue was not settled until about 1820.[11] The Constitution does not state specifically that the judiciary should determine whether national laws were contrary to the Constitution. The Supreme Court claimed that authority in 1803, but it was not used much until after the Civil War.

One indication of the primacy of Congress among the national institutions appears in the provisions for amending the Constitution. Article V provides for proposal by two-thirds of both houses and for ratification by three-fourths of the states. Yet there is no mention of either the president or the Supreme Court. Their participation is limited to whatever informal influence they can have upon the houses of Congress or the states.

The amending process is an adaptation of the theory of common functions. Separated institutions each act on the same question. Proposal is in one set of institutions and ratification in another. Each house of Congress can prevent the proposal of an amendment, and a certain minority of states—one more than a quarter of them—can stop the ratification. This is, of course, a basic recognition of the federal character of our Union. There are less evident indications of federalism, such as the specific style of the grants to Congress. Their specificity suggests that the national government lacks general legislative power.

At the same time, the 1787 Constitution did not repeat the provision of the Articles of the Confederation to the effect that each state retains "every power, jurisdiction and right, which is not by this confederation expressly delegated to the United States, in Congress assembled." The Tenth Amendment to the new Constitution reserves to the states "powers not delegated to the United States," but this was held to allow implied as well as express powers to the national authority.[12] Also, there is a large field of overlapping powers under the 1787 Constitution, and the Supreme Court has held that Congress by first action may preempt a field of jurisdiction. As will be shown, the specific grants to Congress cover considerable areas of both internal and external sovereignty, but there has been definite enlargement of the specific grants by these methods of "broad interpretation."[13]

The supremacy of Congress among the national institutions is evident also in the number of instances in which the Constitution expressly grants Congress authority with respect to the executive and judicial powers. For instance, it gives Congress power to establish executive offices and to stipulate who may appoint the officials. Likewise, it prescribes Congress authority to make exceptions and regulations with respect to the appellate jurisdiction of the Supreme Court. We will discuss other instances in the later section on the non-law-making powers of Congress.

BROAD POWERS OVER INTERNAL SOVEREIGNTY

The most fundamental reason for the Constitutional Convention of 1787, as explained in previous chapters, was the fact that the Articles of Confederation did not provide Congress with sufficient authority, independently of the states, to finance and enforce the conduct of even foreign and interstate relations.[14] The power to tax, regulate commerce, and to prosecute violations were in effect reserved entirely to the states.[15]

The Constitution of 1787 did more than correct the deficiencies of the articles. It also provided authority to enter new fields with respect to both internal and external sovereignty. The next section will set forth the powers of Congress with respect to foreign relations and military affairs. This section will concern internal sovereignty. The breadth of the authority of Congress in this area is evident from the first 9 of the 18 enumerated powers in Section 8 of Article I (the first three also apply to external sovereignty):

> [1] The Congress shall have power to lay and collect taxes, duties, imposts and excises, to pay the debts and provide for the common defence and general welfare of the United States; but all duties, imposts and excises shall be uniform throughout the United States;
>
> [2] To borrow money on the credit of the United States;
>
> [3] To regulate commerce with foreign nations, and among the several States, and with the Indian tribes;
>
> [4] To establish an uniform rule of naturalization, and uniform laws on the subject of bankruptcies throughout the United States;
>
> [5] To coin money, regulate the value thereof, and of foreign coin, and fix the standard of weights and measures;
>
> [6] To provide for the punishment of counterfeiting the securities and current coin of the United States;
>
> [7] To establish post offices and post roads;
>
> [8] To promote the progress of science and useful arts by securing for limited times to authors and inventors the exclusive right to their respective writings and discoveries;
>
> [9] To constitute tribunals inferior to the Supreme Court;

There is the general limitation of what is not authorized and some specific limitations in types and forms of taxes, as well as the specification of the enumerated powers. Yet there are evidences that the Convention, in its final adoptions, had a broad, positive view of government. The delegations saw the value of uniform laws in naturalization and bankruptcy, standard currency, weights and measures, and the promotion of the arts and sciences.

A number of provisions allow considerable discretion in legislation. The first power, with respect to taxes, permits a good deal of discretion despite the general limitations against real property taxes and the requirement of uniformity. The statement of purposes—common defense and general welfare—is not in itself a grant of all the power needed for those ends. The provision is still an authorization of taxes for the purpose stated elsewhere. The power was expanded when Congress began to tax incomes. The Supreme Court held this contrary to the requirements of uniformity, but the Sixteenth Amendment removed that difficulty.[16] During the period 1930-80, the rise in national income tax rates has given the national government considerable advantage over the states in financing welfare for the disadvantaged. Since 1980 this has been reduced, but the states are handicapped in the use of income taxes. Persons can move to another state more easily than they can move to another country. The developments of the 1980s furnish a new test for the ability of certain states to deal with the problems that arise from concentrations of low-income persons.[17]

There are two other enumerated powers that have enlarged the authority of Congress to deal with domestic matters. One of these authorizes Congress to "regulate Commerce with foreign Nations, and among the several States, and with the Indian tribes." This has been used by Congress to enter many of the fields of regulation formerly occupied by the states, as well as many new areas. In this Congress has been aided by the willingness of many courts to give the authorization a broad interpretation. As a result, it applies not only to wares in transit, but also transactions that affect goods that have been or will be in transit.[18]

The explicit authority of Congress to enact "all laws which shall be necessary and proper for carrying into execution" the various powers of the government and its departments and officers is particularly relevant to the principal aim of this book, that is, to explain the group purpose and the common functions of the two houses of Congress and the presidency.

The Constitution implicitly connects the president to this power of Congress by the provision obligating the president to recommend to Congress "such measures as he shall judge necessary and expedient" (Art. II, Sec. iii). This seems designed to bring Congress and the president together in proposing and even formulating what is necessary for executive operations. The grant to Congress refers to what is "necessary and proper for carrying into execution" powers of the government and its units.

Congress is also deeply involved in the establishment and operations of the executive system. This will be shown in Chapter 7, which examines the establishment of the executive departments and agencies. The enumerated powers of Congress suggest structures for the post office, the military, and the navy, but there is no general authorization of executive departments. At its first session Congress set up three departments, presumably under the power to enact necessary laws. Such congressional efforts will be explained in Chapter 7.

BROAD POWERS OVER EXTERNAL SOVEREIGNTY

The U.S. Constitution makers massively rejected the 1690 ideas of the English political theorist, John Locke, that foreign policy cannot be stated in antecedent laws and that such legislative discretion is exercised by the executive under the label of "federative power."[19] The Articles of Confederation granted Congress many items of authority in the foreign and security areas, and the 1787 Constitution, even though introducing the presidency, granted Congress still more authority with respect to these matters. The Constitution is quite specific in granting Congress much authority with respect to foreign relations and military institutions. Pfiffner addresses the Constitutional split of military power:

> The framers purposefully split the military power of the United States between Congress and the president. Neither could control the military apparatus without the other. Congress had the power to mobilize national resources in raising an army and navy, but the president as commander in chief could command the armed forces.
>
> Before 1940 policy conflicts between president and Congress over defense were infrequent. But after 1940 with the increasing importance of defense, particularly the large portion of the national budget consumed by it, Congress has come to play a greater role in defense policy making.[20]

The largest general category of congressional powers concerns foreign/security affairs. Of the 18 enumerated powers in Section 8 of Article I, ten affect this area. These include the first three set forth in the above list of domestic powers, and these seven:

> To define and punish Piracies and Felonies committed on the high Seas, and Offenses against the Law of Nations;
> To declare War, grant Letters of Marque and Reprisal, and make Rules concerning Captures on Land and Water;
> To raise and support Armies, but no Appropriations of Money to that Use shall be for a longer Term than two Years;
> To provide and maintain a Navy;
> To make Rules for the Government and Regulation of the land and naval Forces;
> To provide for calling forth the Militia to execute the Laws of the Union, suppress Insurrections and repel Invasion;
> To provide for organizing, arming, and disciplining the Militia, and for governing such Part of them as may be employed in the Service of the United States, reserving to the States, respectively, the Appointment of the Officers, and the Authority of training the Militia according to the discipline prescribed by Congress;

This list of powers exceeds those granted Congress under the Articles of Confederation. The new authority of Congress to define and punish offences against the law of nations is particularly interesting. This rejects the idea of Locke and Montesquieu that the executive has full power concerning the law of nations.

The most interesting addition to the powers of Congress is the authority to provide for calling forth the militia "to execute the laws of the union, suppress insurrections, and repel invasions." These are matters quite likely to involve the president's duties concerning execution of the laws and command of the armed forces. But the Constitution gives Congress the authority to stipulate when and how the militia may be called forth for these important purposes.

This authorization is related to the next provision for organizing, arming, and disciplining the militia. The militia units are basically state organizations, and the state constitutions made the respective governors or presidents of the states the officer in charge of the militia. Nine state constitutions used the specific term *commander in chief*, and the other two new constitutions used comparable designations. Thus the authority of Congress allows it to determine the military relationships of the presidents and the state governors.

Congress rather promptly used its authority in this regard. It enacted statutes spelling out the conditions under which the president could call out the militia.[21] Accordingly, the authority of the president to use the militia to execute the laws, suppress insurrections, and repel invasions comes from Congress, acting under its constitutional authority, rather than directly to the president from the Constitution. Presidents may indicate that the authority comes from the Constitution, but, in fact, it comes from Congress as Congress determines. Concerning the use of the military, Strum states:

> For all practical purposes, it is irrelevant to argue whether a particular power has been given to Congress or to the President. Each branch recognizes its dependence on the other and usually foregoes action unless it has at least the tacit consent of the other branch.
>
> Congress is entitled to declare war and to raise and regulate the armed forces, but the military commander—the man who actually conducts the war—is the president. The war power is actually divided between the two branches. The Constitution thus necessitates a bargaining process. . . .[22]

Furthermore, Strum elucidates the bargaining process involved:

> As this examination of the war power has shown, the powers that the Constitution gives to the president or to Congress are no more than the authority to do something with the consent, tacit or otherwise, of the other branch. To act alone is to proceed at one's own peril. A president will not usually undertake an important move entirely alone, less out of fear of constitutional limitations than out of his need to protect his bargaining position for the implementation of his entire program.[23]

NON-LAW-MAKING ASSIGNMENTS

The focus of this book upon the mixed functions of the houses of Congress and the presidency is supported by the specification in the Constitution of "non-law-making" rights and duties for the House of Representatives and the Senate. We do not call these non-legislative functions because of the broad meaning often given to the term *legislative*.[24] The non-law-making function of most interest in this study is representation. A leading analyst of Congress gives the following explanation of that responsibility:

Part of a Congressman's job is to represent the people, in all the diversity of their economic, social, and cultural interests, . . . Senators represent the states in their equality, and Representatives the multifarious interests of the people in general. . . . Congress not only represents the states and districts in the national capital; it also informs the folks back home of national and international problems and how these problems affect them.[25]

The most striking non-law-making assignment concerns impeachment and trial. Article II stipulates that the president, vice-president, and all civil officers shall be removed from office upon impeachment and conviction of treason, bribery, or other high crimes and misdemeanors. Article I states that the House has the sole power of impeachment and that the Senate has "the sole power to try all impeachments." Article I also provides that when the president is tried, the chief justice shall preside, and conviction requires the concurrence of two-thirds of the members present.[26]

The role of the houses of Congress in the amendment of the Constitution was explained early in this chapter and will not be considered at this point. The Constitution also authorizes state legislatures to make regulations concerning the times, places, and manner of holding elections for senators and representatives and empowers Congress to make or alter such regulations. That also may be deemed "making law." The Senate must approve treaties made by the president. Opinions conflict on whether treaties are laws, but Chapter 10 demonstrates that they have equal force.

Congress has conditional functions concerning the election of the president and vice-president. Article II provides that if the presidential electoral colleges do not provide a majority vote for the president or vice-president, the House of Representatives shall choose the president and the Senate the vice-president.[27]

Article IV provides that Congress shall have power to make "all needful rules and regulations respecting the territory or other property belonging to the United States."[28]

As described more fully in Chapter 7, the houses of Congress have considerable authority with respect to the establishment and operations of the executive departments and agencies, and that they exercise that power by legislation and investigation.

LIMITATIONS UPON THE POWERS OF CONGRESS

The restrictive force of the Constitution is not limited to such indirect methods as checks and balances or separation of powers. It may and often does take the form of direct limitations. The Constitution has many such restrictions upon the national and state legislatures, principally in the last sections of Article I and in the amendments to the Constitution.[29]

The restrictions affecting the houses of Congress mostly come in the section following the 18 enumerated powers of Congress. They tend to be specific and rather diversified. Each is probably the result of some early controversy including those between national and state forces at the Convention of 1787. Briefly, they are:

> The state importation of persons [slaves] shall not be prohibited prior to 1808.
> Habeas corpus shall not be suspended unless rebellion or invasion cause public safety to require it.
> A bill of attainder or ex post facto law is not allowed.
> Direct taxes must be in proportion to population.
> No duty or tax on imports from any state.
> Regulation of commerce shall not give one state preference over another.
> No money shall be drawn from the Treasury but in consequence of appropriations by law.
> United States shall not grant any title of nobility.
> No officer shall accept anything from King, Prince, or foreign state, without consent of Congress.

There is also a section of limitations upon state legislatures. They prohibit a state from making a treaty or engaging in certain other matters of foreign affairs and from taxing commerce. Also a state may not impair the obligation of contracts. This may be directed against scaling down debts.

These two sets of limitations indicate the extent to which the formulation of the Constitution involved nation-state affairs much more than relations between national institutions.

The Bill of Rights, composed of the first ten amendments, also places substantial limitations upon the operation of the government. The Articles of Confederation had no declaration of rights, but the majority of states with new constitutions had comprehensive bills of rights. In each, at least half of the provisions concerned judicial procedure.

The partial nationalization of internal sovereignty by the 1787 Constitution meant that there would be a national criminal law and probably other coercive proceedings against individuals. During the ratification debates, proponents promised a bill of rights. The first Congress recognized that commitment and proposed 12 amendments for the purpose. Ten were approved by 1791, and they became the Bill of Rights. Five relate to judicial procedure, mostly a criminal law type of process.

The First Amendment explicitly prohibits Congress from passing laws abridging various forms of expression and association. It is also the basis of the political party and the special interest group systems.

NOTES

1. George B. Galloway, *The Legislative Process in Congress* (New York: Crowell, 1953), p. 7.

2. James MacGregor Burns, *Leadership* (New York: Harper & Row, 1978), p. 385.

3. James Madison, *The Federalist Papers—Hamilton—Madison—Jay*, letter no. 51 (New York: New American Library, 1961), p. 322.

4. "THE LEGISLATIVE PROCESS may be broadly defined to include all the functions and activities of the modern legislature: making the laws, supervising the administration, representing and informing the people. It also includes the activities of executive and judicial agencies of government insofar as they share in lawmaking and policy formulation, as well as the part played in this field by political parties, interest groups, and public opinion. Thus broadly conceived, the legislative process embraces all the elements and forces in a democratic society that influence the formulation, enactment, implementation, and review of public policy." Galloway, *Legislative Process*, p. 3.

5. The president "shall from time to time give to the Congress Information of the State of the Union, and recommend to their Consideration such Measures as he shall judge necessary and expedient; he may, on extraordinary occasions, convene both Houses, or either of them, . . . ": *U.S. Const.*, Art. II, Sec. 3. See also chap. 6, "The Chief Legislator."

6. *U.S. Const.*, Art. II, Secs. 1, 2; Art. III, Sec. 2; Art. IV, Sec. 3; Art. V. See C. Herman Pritchett, *The American Constitutional System*, 5th ed. (New York: McGraw-Hill, 1981), p. 36; J. W. Peltason, *Understanding the Constitution*, 9th ed. (New York: Holt, Rinehart, and Winston, 1982), pp. 89, 100, 106, 109-11.

7. *McGrain v. Daugherty*, 273 U.S. 135 (1927). Joseph P. Harris, *Congress and the Legislative Process*, 2nd ed. (New York: McGraw-Hill, 1972), pp. 166–74. Peltason, *Understanding the Constitution*, pp. 70–71.

8. See the chapters on "The Rise of Liberalism," "Utilitarianism," and "Changing Concepts of Law in the Nineteenth and Twentieth Centuries" in John H. Hallowell, *Main Currents in Modern Political Thought* (New York: Henry Holt, 1950), pp. 84–117, 198–234, and 328–67. Galloway, *Legislative Process*, pp. 38–65, 198–225. A. T. Mason and R. H. Leach, *In Quest of Freedom: American Political Thought and Practice* (Englewood Cliffs, N.J.: Prentice-Hall, 1959), pp. 1–25.

9. See Chapters 12 and 14.

10. See Peltason, *Understanding the Constitution*, pp. 113–16.

11. *Martin v. Hunter's Lessee*, 1 Wheat, 304 (1816); *Cohens v. Virginia*, 6 Wheat, 264 (1821). See Rocco J. Tresolini and Martin Shapiro, *American Constitutional Law*, 3rd ed. (New York: Macmillan, 1970), pp. 123–42. A. T. Mason and W. M. Beaney, *American Constitutional Law*, 5th ed. (Englewood Cliffs, N.J.: Prentice-Hall, 1972), p. 108.

12. See Peltason, *Understanding the Constitution*, p. 178.

13. Mason and Beaney, *American Constitutional Law*, pp. 105–9, 163–65, 207–22.

14. See the section entitled, "Need for Partial Nationalization of Internal Sovereignty" in Chapter 2.

15. Edmund S. Morgan, *The Birth of the Republic: 1763–1789* (Chicago: University of Chicago Press, 1956), pp. 121–28.

16. See Peltason, *Understanding the Constitution*, p. 53, 211; Mason and Beaney, *American Constitutional Law*, pp. 273–77.

17. In the 1970s a leading analyst declared "the man in the White House has become the President of the Cities." James MacGregor Burns, *Presidential Government,* Sentry edition (Boston: Houghton Mifflin, 1973), p. 318.

18. The Supreme Court upheld a provision in the Civil Rights Act of 1964 against racial discrimination in hotels. The Court based the decision upon the commerce clause. "The power of Congress to promote interstate commerce also includes the power to . . . prohibit racial discrimination by motels serving travelers, however 'local' their operations may appear." *Heart of Atlanta Motel v. United States,* 379 U.S. 241 (1964).

19. For a contrary view, see Robert Scigliano, "The War Powers Resolution and the War Powers," in Joseph M. Bessette and Jeffrey Tulis, eds., *The Presidency in the Constitutional Order* (Baton Rouge: Lousiana State University Press, 1981), p. 132.

20. James P. Pfiffner, *The President, the Budget, and Congress: Impoundment and the 1974 Budget Act* (Boulder, Colo.: Westview Press, 1979), p. 70.

21. *The Public Statutes at Large of the United States of America*, vol. 1 (Boston: Little, Brown, 1854), pp. 264–65.

22. Philippa Strum, *Presidential Power and American Democracy* 3d ed. (Santa Monica, Calif.: Goodyear, 1979), p. 13.

23. Ibid., pp. 14, 21.

24. See note 4.

25. Galloway, *Legislative Process,* p. 198.

26. Peltason, *Understanding the Constitution,* pp. 40, 41, 92.

27. Ibid., pp. 81–82.

28. Ibid., p. 107.

29. *U.S. Const.,* Art. I, Secs. 10, 11; Peltason, *Understanding the Constitution,* pp. 71–77.

6

The President in
the Constitution

The Constitution places the president in a political system that hedges
him about with limits and restraints. It specifies how presidents are
to be chosen and, if necessary, removed. It creates a Congress, with
"all legislative powers," and a coordinate judicial branch; and it provides a variety of checks and balances by which each branch can limit
the others. Moreover, it restricts the power of the whole federal
government to what is specifically enumerated and leaves the rest to
the states or the people.

Benjamin I. Page and Mark P. Petracca[1]

The process of government requires that these separate institutions
work together with some measure of effective cooperation, and this
is perhaps the key problem of the constitutional system of the United
States.

C. Herman Pritchett[2]

To ask what is to become of the presidency is to ask what is to become of the entire American political order.

Grant McConnell[3]

A number of scholarly analysts assert that there are two presidencies. In most instances, this means domestic and foreign.[4] In a
few cases, it refers to passive and active types.[5] This book does not
try to divide the presidency in any such way. It is more concerned
with bringing the president and the two houses of Congress together

and recognizing that this group is a public policy superstructure with common responsibilities in the legislative, executive, and representational functions of the government.

At the Constitutional Convention,[6] the Virginia Plan proposed a "national executive," apparently to function between the "national legislative" and the "national judiciary."[7] But the midconvention draft constitution proposed a "President of the United States" with a variety of rights and duties.[8]

This chapter will explain these two points of view and also examine how the presidency may develop into an office of central leadership in the executive, legislative, and representational realms. The application and adaptation of the various powers of the president will be examined in Chapter 9.

THE DIVERSE FUNCTIONS OF THE PRESIDENCY

The contrast between the single idea at the start of Article II and multiple provisions of its inner structure is more than the difference between one and a dozen. Basically, the first is a legal function, and the other is the many-sided involvement of a high policy leader.

The preceding chapter explained the many differences between law making and the total operations of the houses of Congress. This chapter examines the contrast of "executive power" in the essentially coercive process of government and the diverse public-image activities of an elected personality whose principal effort is to get on top of his relations with both the vast public and the conglomerate government. Moreover, the latter is not merely a complex executive system, but also a loosely organized legislative system, and a threefold representational branch that has never been near the thought of unified organization.

Article II starts with the idea that the "executive power" is vested in a president of the United States. The constitution does not explain "executive power," except to suggest that it is something between "legislative power" and "judicial power."[9] In Sections 2 and 3 there is an itemization of rights and duties, but these do not expressly relate to "executive power" but rather explicitly concern "the President."[10] Some analysts of the U.S. national government assume that "executive power" and "the President" are synonymous,[11] but we have seen that the Constitution gives the president a number of roles beyond the execution of legislation. Also, three-power government may be a limited concept of government.

The first question is what is the general character of the several prescriptions in Sections 2 and 3 of Article II. To aid in that endeavor, their 12 subjects will be shown:

[1] The President shall be Commander-in-Chief of the Army and Navy of the United States, and of the militia of the several States when called into the actual service of the United States;

[2] he may require the opinion, in writing, of the principal officer in each of the executive departments, upon any subject relating to the duties of their respective offices, and

[3] he shall have power to grant reprieves and pardons for offenses against the United States, except in cases of impeachment.

[4] He shall have power, by and with the advice and consent of the Senate, to make treaties, provided two-thirds of the Senators present concur; and

[5] he shall nominate, and, by and with the advice and consent of the Senate, shall appoint ambassadors, other public ministers and consuls, judges of the Supreme Court, and all other officers of the United States whose appointments are not herein otherwise provided for, and which shall be established by law; but

[6] the Congress may by law vest the appointment of such inferior officers, as they think proper, in the President alone, in the courts of law, or in the heads of departments.

[7] The President shall have power to fill up all vacancies that may happen during the recess of the Senate, by granting commissions which shall expire at the end of their next session.

[8] He shall from time to time give to the Congress information of the state of the Union, and recommend to their consideration such measures as he shall judge necessary and expedient;

[9] he may, on extraordinary occasions, convene both Houses, or either of them, and in case of disagreement between them with respect to the time of adjournment, he may adjourn them to such time as he shall think proper;

[10] he shall receive ambassadors and other public ministers;

[11] he shall take care that the laws be faithfully executed; and

[12] [he] shall commission all the officers of the United States.

This is a diverse list of rights and duties. What the several functions have most in common is the direct or indirect dependence upon some action by Congress. For instance, the president is designated commander in chief, and, as the preceding chapter showed, the military power is divided between Congress and the president. Likewise, treaty-making power is dependent upon the approval of the Senate.

Other instances will be considered later: those on appointments in Chapter 7, the relationships with Congress in the section of this chapter on the chief legislator, and that concerning execution of laws will be discussed in the next section.

THE CHIEF EXECUTIVE

The introductory sentence of Article II says that "executive power" is vested in the president. Two immediate comments seem pertinent. First, the 12 rights and duties listed in the last section include several functions that are not executive in character, such as granting reprieves. That may be monarchical, but it is not the execution of a law, rule, or order.

The president is expressly obligated to "take care that the laws be faithfully executed." That would seem to connect the president to the execution of laws and to require action faithful to the legislative intent of Congress. This provision is similar to provisions in a number of state constitutions adopted before 1787 and to have its origin in the English Bill of Rights of 1689.[12] That background suggests the principle that the executive should not suspend execution without the consent of the legislature. The English declaration followed the parliamentary ouster of James II, who had refused to apply anti-Catholic laws, but it had a broader meaning.[13] As a constitutional principle, it meant the supremacy of the legislative over the executive. For the American colonists, that meant the supremacy of their assembly over the London-appointed governors. When the new American states wrote constitutions, the principle of nonsuspension appeared in several declarations of rights.

Eleven states, acting mostly through their legislatures, adopted new constitutions, as previously noted. Seven of these were accompanied by separate, comprehensive bills of rights. Six of these included paragraphs against unauthorized executive suspension.[14] The exception was Pennsylvania, which did not have a single chief executive, such as a governor. Rather it had an executive council of 12 elected members, the president of which was merely first among equals.[15]

The states with nonsuspension declarations included Virginia and Massachusetts. They were in many ways the leaders in the constitution movement. Their provisions against suspension were similar:

> Sec. 7. That all power of suspending laws, or the execution of laws, by any authority, without consent of the representatives of the people, is injurious to their rights, and ought not to be exercised [Virginia].

> Art. XX. The power of suspending laws, or the execution of the laws, ought never to be exercised but by the legislature, or by authority derived from it, to be exercised in such particular cases only as the legislature shall expressly provide for [Massachusetts].[16]

These provisions are essentially similar, and, moreover, they are much like the declaration in the English Bill of Rights of 1689.

The most interesting aspect of the similarity of the Virginia and Massachusetts provisions against suspension is that in one case the governor was chosen by the legislature, and in the other he was elected by the general voters. Thus the principle of legislative superiority to execution obtains equally whether the governor was elected by the people or chosen by the legislature.

The limitations upon execution in the other four declarations of rights were similar to those of Virginia and Massachusetts. In fact, the clause in North Carolina was identical to the Virginia one, and that of New Hampshire was the same as the one in Massachusetts. The provisions for Delaware and Maryland were much alike, and both were similar to the ones quoted above.

The only state other than Massachusetts and New Hampshire to have a popularly elected governor was New York. Its constitution was not accompanied by a separate, comprehensive declaration of rights. But there were some limitations worked into the body of the constitution proper. The New York constitution may be of particular significance because it may have been the source of many provisions in the U.S. Constitution with respect to the presidency. There is one paragraph in the New York constitution that seems particularly relevant to the developments at the 1787 convention in Philadelphia:

> XIX. That it shall be the duty of the governor to inform the legislature, at every session, on the condition of the State, so far as may respect his department; to recommend such matters to their

consideration as shall appear to him to concern its good government, welfare, and prosperity; to correspond with the Continental Congress, and other States; to transact all necessary business with the officers of government, civil and military, *to take care that the laws are faithfully executed to the best of his ability;* and to expedite all such measures, as may be resolved upon by the legislature [Emphasis added].[17]

The italicized clause is much like a provision in the U.S. Constitution. The primacy of the legislature is evident in both.

The obligation of executive officials to Congress may be implicit in another constitution provision. This says that the president may require the opinion, in writing, of the principal officer in each of the executive departments, upon any relevant subject. This is sometimes said to make the president the chief of the executive branch, but it would seem to have the contrary inference. If the departments' heads were "the president's men," such a provision would be unnecessary. It seems to suggest that the department officials are, in general, responsive to some other institution, which would be the Congress.

The general conclusion from these various provisions is that the separate action of the executive is not complete independence. The executive is limited by the legislated statute; the legislative and executive powers are interdependent. The executive is free to execute, but he must be faithful to the enactment of the legislature.

THE CHIEF LEGISLATOR

The Constitution did not directly and immediately make the president the chief legislator of the national government. At the convention the American Founders still remembered a good deal of their colonial experience. They had not forgotten that legislative assemblies elected by the people had been the main line of general defense against the governors appointed by London.

The state constitutions of 1776–84 generally did not give the governors much authority. The state assemblies embodied whatever democracy there was. The attitude was much the same at the 1787 convention at Philadelphia. But there was some improvement. The president is allowed at least a qualified veto and is required to supply information and recommendations. The New York constitution may have been the guide, and it was less antigovernor than most other charters. The governor of New York was elected for a three-year term, and Governor Clinton had been reelected a number of times.[18]

The main point about the Constitutional Convention is that attitudes toward legislative-executive relationships were changing and that they would continue to change. A constitution that reflects the view of the people grows and adapts to the changing demands and interests of the groups within the national society. The 1787 Constitution began to change almost at once, and in a few years it underwent many high-level changes.

Columbia Professor H. L. McBain's *The Living Constitution* of 1927 gives us a picture of relevant developments. He says that the provision vesting executive power in a president "is gentle fraud upon ourselves."[19] He explains that:

> The prime function of the President is not executive at all. It is legislative.
>
> True enough the constitution vests "all legislative powers" in Congress. It purports to withdraw the President from his major executive role and to put him upon the legislative stage in only three minor and exceptional roles. He may call Congress in extraordinary sessions; he may deliver messages; he may veto proposals of law which, if Congress is still in session, may be passed over his veto by a two-thirds vote of each house. Popular demand for the appearance of the President in these lesser parts leaves him little time to star as Chief Executive. Politics has transformed his minor into his major role. The exceptions to his activities as Chief Executive are more important than the constitutional rule.
>
> Moreover, this transformation, this inversion, of the office did not wait the slow progress of time. *The presidency was birth-marked for change in this respect as it came into being.* No President who has, for whatever cause, attempted to self-abnegate himself as leader in the legislative program of Congress and to immolate himself upon the altar of executive duty has been aught but relatively ineffectual [Emphasis added].[20]

Thus Professor McBain finds the basis of the legislative president in the 1787 Constitution itself. Moreover, he says, the ineffectiveness of presidents who put executive action before legislative program is no "cause for wonderment." The policies that "enlist popular interest are mainly legislative" ones. Also, if presidential campaigns have "clear-cut issues of policy," they are legislative. "We elect the President as a leader of legislation. We hold him accountable for what he succeeds in getting Congress to do and in preventing Congress from doing."[21] McBain makes his conclusion quite definite:

> The President, then, is a Chief Legislator rather than a Chief Executive. Moreover, this results not only from the practice of politics but also from law. The constitution vests executive power in the President. But Congress vests executive power nearly everywhere except in the President. Whenever an office is created its powers and duties are determined by statute. The incumbents of executive offices look to the law, not to the President, for the source and scope of their authorities. . . .[22]

Scholarly support for these views is expressed by Professor Wilfred E. Binkley in his 1958 book *The Man in the White House.*[23] He observes that "the citizen, as a voter, scarcely shows any consciousness whatever of the president's executive function, but instead manifests a quadrennial concern as to the legislation the presidential candidates, if elected, may promote or oppose."[24]

There is also proof of Professor McBain's idea that the Constitution itself opens the door to the president as legislator in the regime of George Washington. As the next chapter shows, Alexander Hamilton, backed by the president, engaged in very active leadership of important legislation with respect to taxes and banking.

OTHER ASSIGNMENTS OF THE PRESIDENT

The Constitution prescribes several roles for the president that may not be either legislative or executive. The function of commander in chief will be considered executive even in the sense of applying laws enacted by Congress. Military action may not require a declaration of war, but it does depend upon appropriations and other acts of Congress.

The authority to make treaties with approval of the Senate may involve actions that are legislative or executive or both. Yet treaty making has distinctive aspects. *The Federalist Paper* no. 75 (Hamilton) asserts that treaty making is neither executive nor legislative, but is a "distinct department."[25] It is also unusual in requiring approval by only the Senate. Yet the application of a treaty may require appropriations, and this gives both houses a chance to act for or against. One of the first major conflicts in presidential-congressional relationships arose when the House of Representatives was considering appropriations for the Jay Treaty of 1794.[26]

The third of the quoted roles of the presidency is another function that seems to be neither legislative nor executive. This is the special authority to grant reprieves and pardons. It may be a traditional monarchical or gubernatorial right, and it does not come between legislation and adjudication. Indeed, it comes still later and may be a check upon the judicial system. It is a reminder that the presidency is the republican successor to kingship.

The role of receiving ambassadors and other public ministers is not executive in the sense of applying congressional legislation; it is more a sovereign function of the head of state. The Articles of Confederation gave Congress the right to appoint and receive ambassadors. That was making a legislative council the successor to the monarchical right to deal with the representatives of other nations. The Constitution divides that right between appointment, which it gives to the president with approval of the Senate, and the reception of ambassadors, which it assigns to the president. Receiving the representatives of another nation may be a formality, but it could also mean that the other country is diplomatically and even politically recognized as a sovereign member of the family of nations. That may be a decision of considerable substance.

Another function of the president that is mainly formal but might at times become quite important is the authority to commission all officers of the United States. Most of the time this is a formality performed by a mechanical signing machine.

THE SHORT-TERM SOVEREIGN PERSONALITY

The foremost contribution of the American Founders to the theory and practice of constitutional limitation may well be the short term for chief executives. Again, this idea is more implicit than expressed in the Constitution. In addition, the pattern was set in the state constitutions of 1776 and 1780 more than in the federal constitution of 1787. The attitude toward state executives reflected some of the old antagonism toward colonial governors.

During the colonial period, comparatively short terms for representative legislators had become almost a tradition in England and America, while executive officials continued to serve for life or for the pleasure of the monarch.

Chapter 2 showed that some of the new state bills of rights had bracketed executives with legislators rather than with judges. That tended to bring at least chief executives under the protective principle of short terms. The new state constitutions gave most governors terms of one or two years.

The 1787 convention first voted the national executive one seven-year term. The package of revisions during the final two weeks included four-year terms without express limit. But, more importantly, the midconvention draft constitution, as noted, had introduced the office of "President of the United States" with a range of functions that gave it several of the attributes of a sovereign monarch despite the limitation of the short term.

The presidency, from the start, has been a national public policy symbol of unity and strength. It had two main sources. In person, the model was retired General George Washington. He had been a symbol of sovereign stature since 1775 when he was chosen commander in chief of the army by the Second Continental Congress. That body was a not very efficient gathering of state delegates. By accepting the symbolic leadership of a father figure, the Congress established an arrangement that brought national freedom and sovereignty. The other source of the 1787 symbol was the office of the president of the Confederation Congress. That supplied the title and also the idea of an elevated first among equals.

President Washington filled the place left by the English monarch and assured that the president would be chief of state. We are designating the position that of a "Short-Term Sovereign Personality," which combines a number of attributes.

This study has at times suggested that the president was the chief representative, but it may be more accurate to use "personality" than "representative." In 1787 representation was associated with areas or states rather than with the whole nation. The colonists complained that they were not represented in the English government. They did not consider the king or a governor to be a representative. The concept of representation may have broadened since then, but even now for many citizens the president personifies the sovereign nation.

Support for the idea that the president of the United States is the chief/personality for the constitutional system appeared in an article in the *Yale Review* more than 60 years ago. The article is entitled "Presidential Leadership" and asserts that "the President is the one official whose position marks him at the present time as the national leader."[27] Congress is under the "sway of organization." The following explanation is given: "There is nothing in the nature of Congress that invites national leadership; or in its organization and machinery that compels it; or in the procedure that demands it. Besides, committees do not invent; they dissect."[28] Many present-day analysts also contend that Congress is not capable of providing strong national leadership. For that, Congress must look to the president. In this situation, however, the leader is not in the position of an orchestra conductor. The members of Congress are not ready to perform as one in conformity to the musical score and the baton of the conductor. There are many who can be led only by strategem and political skill and force. The president, to lead Congress, will need much capacity in "coordinative politics," as well as skill and stamina. The article describes the attitude of the ordinary citizen:

> The phrase "a Constitutional President," therefore, means various things. It means to the Senators and Representatives a President who recommends what they want and appoints whom they wish. . . . But to the average citizen, engrossed in his daily affairs and not in the least interested in technical distinctions, it means a President who adapts the stupendous powers of his office to the needs of the hour.
>
> The average man feels like this for several reasons. In the first place, the President is the only officer in the government elected by the whole country. He is, in a very real sense, everybody's representative, because everybody votes for him, or against him—and psychologically this amounts to the same thing. When, therefore, an emergency demands immediate action, the average citizen expects the President to take action. He doesn't stop to ask whether the Constitution empowers the President to do so.[29]

The average citizen's concept of the presidency may be actually quite sophisticated. In an emergency, the president is to act, without thought of the legal question. That issue is for Congress to consider after the action and then ratify or not as it thinks proper. The Constitutional Convention denied the president any "prerogative" to decide himself what is right. This book adopts that position and assigns the president the duty of action. It may be called "preaction." The action comes before the Congress decides whether the action has legal basis. The reaction of the average citizen may be the best solution to this problem of how a slow-acting Congress may control a fast-acting president.

NOTES

1. Benjamin I. Page and Mark P. Petracca, *The American Presidency* (New York: McGraw-Hill, 1983) p. 19.

2. C. Herman Pritchett, *The American Constitutional System*, 5th ed. (New York: McGraw-Hill, 1981), p. 29.

3. Grant McConnell, *The Modern Presidency*, 2d ed. (New York: St. Martin's Press, 1976), p. 100.

4. Aaron Wildavsky, "The Two Presidencies," in Aaron Wildavsky, ed., *The Presidency* (Boston: Little, Brown, 1969), pp. 230–243. One basis of distinction is congressional approval of presidential proposals. The difference seems relative. The percentage of approval on domestic policies is 40.2 percent, on foreign is 58.5 percent, and on defense is 73.3 percent. See also Dorothy James, *The Contemporary Presidency*, 2d ed. (Indianapolis: Bobbs-Merrill, 1974), pp. 176, 227; Philippa Strum, *Presidential Power and American Democracy*, 2d ed. (Santa Monica, Calif.: Goodyear, 1979), p. 165.

5. For instance, Jeffrey Tulis, "The Two Constitutional Presidencies," in Michael Nelson, ed., *The Presidency and the Political System* (Washington, D.C.: Congressional Quarterly Press, 1984), pp. 59–86.

6. See Chapters 3 and 4.

7. *Notes of Debates in the Federal Convention of 1787 Reported by James Madison* (New York: Norton, 1966), p. 34 (hereafter cited as *Madison's Notes*).

8. Ibid., pp. 392–93.

9. *U.S. Const.*, Arts. I, II, III (first sentence of each).

10. Ibid., Art. II, Secs. 2, 3.

11. "The more general view, and the one that conforms to presidential practices, is that this section [which vests executive power in a president] gives the President a power that has never been defined or enumerated and, in fact, cannot be defined since its scope depends largely upon circumstances." J. W. Peltason, *Understanding the Constitution*, 9th ed. (New York: Holt, Rinehart and Winston, 1982), p. 78. This book says that this viewpoint may pertain to presidential power but not to executive power. This last means the authority to execute legislated statutes and is limited by the enactments of Congress. Presidential power may not be limited in this way.

12. Carl Stephenson and Frederick G. Marcham, *Sources of English Constitutional History* (New York: Harper & Bros., 1937), p. 601.

13. Colin Lovell, *English Constitutional and Legal History* (New York: Oxford University Press, 1962), pp. 389–94.

14. Delaware, Maryland, Massachusetts, New Hampshire, North Carolina, Virginia. Benjamin Perley Poore, ed., *The Federal and State Constitutions,*

Colonial Charters, and other Organic Laws of the United States (Washington, D.C.: Government Printing Office, 1877), pp. 918, 959, 1283, 1409, 1909.

15. Ibid., pp. 1544–45.

16. Henry S. Commager, ed., *Documents of American History*, 5th ed. (New York: Appleton-Century-Crofts, 1949), pp. 104, 109.

17. Poore, *Federal and State Constitutions,* p. 1335.

18. George Clinton was elected to six consecutive terms, 1777–95.

19. Howard Lee McBain, *The Living Constitution* (New York: Workers Education Bureau Press, 1927), pp. 115.

20. Ibid., pp. 115–16.

21. Ibid., p. 116.

22. Ibid., pp. 117–18.

23. Wilfred E. Binkley, *The Man in the White House*, rev. ed. (New York: Harper & Row, 1958), p. 133.

24. Ibid., p. 132–33.

25. *The Federalist Papers* (New York: New American Library, 1961), letter no. 75, pp. 450–51.

26. Joseph Charles, *The Origins of the American Party System* (New York: Harper & Row, 1956), pp. 110–22.

27. Samuel P. Orth, "Presidential Leadership," *Yale Review* 10 (April 1921):453.

28. Ibid., p. 454.

29. Ibid., p. 455.

PART II

ADAPTATION OF
THE CONSTITUTIONAL SYSTEM

THE GROWTH OF THE REPRESENTATIONAL PYRAMID

Part I of this book explained the formation of our constitutional system, with particular emphasis upon the potentials of Congress and the presidency to develop into a representational group and a public policy superstructure. Part II will continue that account, with primary attention to the development of the Congress and the presidency into their present state of common responsibility for the legislative, executive, and representational systems.

The primary theme throughout Part II will be the diversification of the functions of Congress and the presidency and the manner in which these institutions developed a mixed guidance and scrutiny of the legislative and executive systems.

Chapter 7 will describe the extent to which the first Congresses continued the work of the Constitutional Convention and established the executive and judicial branches as well as providing for the structures and procedures of Congress itself.

Chapters 8 and 9 will discuss the principal changes in the priorities of Congress and the presidents, respectively. Emphasis will be placed on the extent to which Congress has become much more decentralized in organization and upon the growth of the representational pyramid of the U.S. national government.

Chapters 10 and 11 will deal with the shared responsibilities of the Congress and the presidency in the areas of legislation and legitimation. They will explain the attitudes of the Supreme Court toward the interactions between the elected institutions, particularly the Court's support of congressional delegations of authority to the president and the Court's rejection of presidential independence even in times of war.

7

Congressional Establishment of the Constitutional System

The Constitution of the United States places Congress at the core of the American political system by vesting all legislative power in its two houses. . . . Plainly, the Founding Fathers intended that the broad mission of the new government was to be charted by the national legislature.

William J. Keefe[1]

The framers of the Constitution left the finality of decision making where they put the greater part of the popular sovereignty—in the Congress. Congress has delegated a great many powers to the executive, and in return required its legatees to report what they propose to do or what they have already done under their derived power.

John Helmer[2]

Once the Constitution of 1787 had been adopted, it needed most to be supplemented and implemented. The convention at Philadelphia, as has been shown, had paid much attention to the basic framework of institutions and authorizations to deal with the immediate difficulties of the existing Confederation system.

The houses of the new Congress had to establish their own patterns of operations as well as the structures of the presidency, the judiciary, and the executive branch.[3] Likewise, Congress needed to enact statutes for national taxation, regulation, enforcement, and other necessary and proper elements of a legal infrastructure.

Legislation with respect to establishment of the executive and judicial systems would be virtually organic in character because of the extent to which the convention left matters to the discretion of the Congress.

This chapter will describe the establishment of these subsystems. The effect of these developments upon the priorities of Congress and the presidency will be examined in the next two chapters.

THE ADOPTION OF CONGRESSIONAL-EXECUTIVE PRACTICES

When the First Congress met in 1789, there had been 15 years of experience in congressional direction of civilian and military officials. The First Continental Congress met in 1774, and the second one served from 1775 to 1781.[4] The Congress of the Confederation began in 1781 and continued until the new Constitution took effect.

All of these Congresses, as well as the Constitutional Convention itself, had been assemblies of state delegates. But they had dealt with the finances, interstate relations, the government of the territories, foreign policies, and military affairs. They had also established various offices and committees. In 1775 the Continental Congress had appointed Benjamin Franklin to be the first postmaster general and George Washington to be commander in chief of the Continental Armies.[5] The Confederation Congress in 1781 established executive departments for finances, foreign relations, and military affairs. In general, each had a single head. After Robert Morris left the financial office, it was directed by a three-man commission. Foreign affairs was headed by Robert Livingston and then by John Jay.[6] Wilfred Binkley's volume on Congress and the president says that Jay often appeared on the floor of the Congress in advising the members and "became virtually the Chief Executive of the government."[7] In fact, in Binkley's assessment he was more successful for a longer period than was Alexander Hamilton during the 1790s.[8]

The relations of the Confederation Congress and the executive departments were so successful that the Constitutional Convention apparently assumed that they would be continued. Professor Binkley says that the First Congress was faced with the following problem:

> How is the administrative organization to be geared to the governmental machine or, more concretely, what is to be the relation between the executive departments and the principal political organs, the President, the House of Representatives, and the Senate?[9]

Binkley states that the debates at the convention "throw almost no light on the matter" but that contemporary correspondence reveals an assumption that the departments would be continued and the principal officers reappointed.[10]

President Washington, Binkley indicates, wished to continue Robert Morris as head of finances and John Jay in charge of foreign affairs. Morris wanted to be outside and Jay preferred to head the judiciary. However, the latter served as head of the new State Department for several months until Thomas Jefferson was available. Then Jay was named the first chief justice of the Supreme Court.[11]

There was definite continuity in the department of military affairs. Henry Knox, a general during the war, held that office for four years at the end of the Confederation and then for four years under the new Constitution. Some second-level officials also continued.[12]

ACTS OF CONGRESS ON MILITARY AFFAIRS, 1789-97

The most essential element of a constitutional democracy is assembly-made law. A political leader and an aristocratic council may be helpful, or even necessary, but the more vital element of a democracy is the participation of an assembly representing the diverse areas of the society in the enactment of statutes that guide executive and judicial action.[13]

When the new central government began to operate in 1789,[14] the superior institution was the House of Representatives. It alone combined the process of direct representation of the people of the states and the process of enacting statutes. It stood above the Senate even though that body represented the equality of the states. In fact, the House probably kept the Senate from being an executive council or cabinet by leading the move to allow the president to remove high officials without Senate approval.

Apparently, there were close relationships between the House and the president during the Washington terms, with some exception for the Third Congress, which had a majority of Republicans.

Congress began at once to enact legislation. The first year it passed 26 acts,[15] and the First Congress adopted a total of 94 statutes.[16] During the Washington presidency, the four Congresses passed nearly 320 acts, 10 percent of which concerned military affairs.[17] In some acts Congress specified the conditions under which the president could call out the militia.

Congress, at its first session, brought the military forces established under the Confederation Congress under the control of the new system. A statute declared that "the establishment of the troops contained in the resolve of the late Congress of Oct. 3, 1787 is hereby recognized to be the establishment for the troops in the service of the United States." In this connection, Congress expressly changed the mode of appointing officers to the president, and it included obedience to the president in the oath of allegiance.[18]

Congress also continued the rules and articles of war established by the preceding Congress. It authorized the president to call into service, from time to time, such part of the militia as he judged "necessary" to protect the inhabitants of the frontiers. This seems pertinent to the basic issue of congressional-presidential relationships because Congress did not leave the establishment of the military order to the constitutional designation of the president to be commander in chief. Rather, Congress expressly authorized by statute the order of military organization and regulation.

Each of the four Congresses of the Washington years enacted at least one statute authorizing the president to exercise discretion in military affairs.[19] Thus the military authority of the president derives from both constitutional stipulation and the statutory enactments by Congress.

STATUTORY FOUNDATION OF
THE NATIONAL INFRASTRUCTURE

The principal operating inadequacy of the Confederation system of 1781-87 was the lack of authority in its Congress to impose and collect taxes, to regulate commerce, and to impose criminal penalties upon individuals within the member states. As noted in previous chapters, all of the internal sovereignty of the United States was in the states and their governments.

The new Congress of 1789 moved quickly to provide the new government with an effective infrastructure. This involved the adoption of public acts with respect to taxation, regulation, criminal liability, the judiciary, and the military. There were 133 statutes in these areas during the eight years of the Washington era.

The second public act, approved July 4, 1789, imposed taxes upon individual persons and levied duties in imported goods, wares, and merchandise. The needs were declared to be threefold: "for the support of the government, for the discharge of the debts of the United States, and thirdly for the encouragement and protection of manufacturers." That first taxing statute listed more than 75 types of items, beginning with distilled spirits, and including many types of tea.[20] If the founders opposed taxation without representation, they clearly favored taxation with representation.

Four of the 26 statutes during the first session of Congress dealt with the imposition and collection of duties. There were 7 more acts in the second and third sessions of the First Congress that dealt with taxes and their collection. The Second Congress adopted 6 others, the Third, 15, and the Fourth, 11, or a total of 43 taxing laws in the first four Congresses.[21] The subjects of taxation were not only imported goods but also tonnage, the use of carriages, and the manufacturing of distilled spirits. This last led to the Whiskey Rebellion, which will be discussed in more detail below.

Regulation was another area in which the new Congress took action involving enforcement. It concerned coastwise vessels, and the exportation of slaves, uninspected articles, firearms, and other items. There was also regulation of coinage. Regulation then was much less than it was a hundred years later, but there were 18 such acts during the years 1789–97.[22]

There was only one statute imposing criminal penalties during the life of the First Congress, but it was extensive. It had 35 sections, including 6 that defined offenses against the law of nations, such as murder and robbery on the high seas. There was no express reference to the law of nations, but several offenses were within its general orbit. The Second, Third, and Fourth Congresses adopted eight criminal laws of a lesser scope.[23]

The most outstanding statute adopted at the first session of the First Congress was the Judiciary Act of 1789. It was a masterpiece of 20 pages, constitutional in character, drafted by a group of experienced legislators and lawyers, the leader of which was Oliver

Ellsworth. He had been an outstanding delegate at the convention, as noted in Chapter 4, and he later became chief justice of the Supreme Court.[24] The Judiciary Act of 1789 dealt with issues left unanswered by the convention, such as whether there would be courts inferior to the Supreme Court, what the scope of the appellate jurisdiction of the Supreme Court would be, and what the relation of the state and national judiciaries would be.

The act established a general pattern of district and circuit courts that has remained to this day. It authorized a number of "district" courts, which are mostly trial courts, and a smaller number of "circuit" courts, which are essentially appellate courts. This meant that the national judiciary would be concerned with more than the constitutionality of legislation, state or national. It made the court system a means of enforcing, or adjudicating, conflicts relating to the public acts concerning taxes and regulations. It was designed to be an important part of the national infrastructure in the enforcement of extractive and regulative statutes.

Section 25 of the Judiciary Act spelled out the jurisdiction with respect to state laws and decisions that might contravene the Constitution of the United States. Article VI of the Constitution suggests that the state judges would determine such questions. But the United States Supreme Court, on the basis of the provisions in the Judiciary Act of Congress, eventually determined that it, rather than state courts, was final in these matters. The conflict was not settled until about 1820, but it was a victory then for the Supreme Court of the United States. The Court in 1803 elevated its image by declaring an act of Congress contrary to the Constitution. But judicial review of national laws did not become sizable until after the Civil War.[25]

The provision of the 1787 Constitution that most assured the new central government a strong infrastructure was the fifteenth enumerated power. This authorized Congress "to provide for calling forth the militia to execute the laws of the Union, suppress insurrections, and repel invasions." It seems noteworthy, first of all, for the combination of subjects. It treats execution of laws, suppression of insurrections, and the repulsion of invasions, as related subjects. Secondly, these are matters where the president would seem to be the first to be aware of necessities and to be able to judge their scope. But the Constitution does not place this responsibility in the president, even as the commander in chief. Rather it places the tests for calling out the militia for these purposes in the bicameral Congress.

The Second Congress, on May 2, 1792, granted the president conditional authority to call out the militia for such purposes. Thus, the president has authority in these matters by virtue of an act of Congress. With respect to invasion, imminent or actual, the presidential authority involves a discretionary decision. He is to judge what is "necessary" to repel the invasion.[26]

With respect to the suppression of insurrections, there are more restrictive conditions. The president may act on application of the state authorities, and he may call forth such number as he deems sufficient. With respect to opposition to the laws of the United States, the president may act when the obstruction is too powerful for the ordinary course of judicial proceedings or for the powers vested in the marshals. The conditions entail notification by a judge. Such conditions were involved in the action against the Whiskey Rebellion in 1794, as will be shown below.[27]

CONGRESSIONAL ESTABLISHMENT OF PRESIDENTIAL-DEPARTMENTAL RELATIONSHIPS

The elevated group character of the elected institutions is evident in the extent to which the houses of Congress exercise control over the relationships of the president and the departments of the executive system. The increasing tendency of the elected institutions to be absorbed in high policy making is seen also in the elevation of the presidents from administrative relations to congressional and public relations.

Chapter 5 noted the scope of the legislative powers of Congress with respect to domestic and foreign affairs, including the authority to enact laws "necessary and proper" for the execution of governmental powers.

While there is no explicit authority to establish executive structures,[28] the Constitution sets forth the following three provisions that refer specifically to "departments."

> The Congress shall have the power . . . To make all laws which shall be necessary and proper for carrying into execution the foregoing powers, and all other powers vested by the Constitution in the government of the United States, or in any department or officer thereof [Art. I, Sec. 8] .

The President may require the opinion, in writing, of the principal officer in each of the executive departments, upon any subject relating to the duties of their respective offices [Art. II, Sec. 2].

. . . the Congress may by law vest the appointment of such inferior officers, as they think proper, in the President alone, in the courts of law, or in the heads of departments [Art. II, Secs. 1, 2].

The Constitution does not refer to "superior" officers, but they would seem to be those officers, such as ambassadors and judges, whose appointment requires approval by the Senate.

The first dozen public acts approved by Congress at its first session included the establishment of departments for foreign affairs, war, and the treasury. Thus Congress more or less continued the three departments established by the Confederation in 1781. Within two months Congress gave the foreign affairs department duties of keeping records for the sovereign government and changed the name to Department of State.[29]

The newly constituted departments differed with respect to relationships of their officials and the presidency and Congress. Two of the departments, State and War, were designated "executive departments," and the president was authorized by statute to enjoin or entrust duties "agreeable to the Constitution," relative to correspondence, commissions, or instructions to or with public ministers or consuls, in the case of the State Department, and comparable matters in the case of the Department of War.

It is Congress that prescribes the authority of the executive departments, such as State or Defense. Congress cannot act contrary to the Constitution, of course, but there are few if any such limitations. The constitutional position of the executive president is to carry out the authorizations prescribed by Congress.

The Treasury Department was another matter. First of all, the act of Congress did not designate it to be an "executive" department, and, in fact, it prescribed close relations between that department and the houses of Congress. This exception is not unusual. Several state legislatures appointed the state treasurer. In fact, the draft constitution at the Philadelphia convention proposed that Congress appoint the national treasurer.[30]

The establishment statute specified more officials and more duties for the Treasury Department. It called for not only the secretary of the treasury and an assistant secretary, but also for a comptroller, an auditor, a treasurer, and a register. Moreover, the statute specified a number of duties for such officials. For instance, the treasurer was required to submit certain reports annually to the houses of Congress.[31] Also, the secretary of the treasury was obligated to prepare for Congress "plans for the improvement and management of the revenue, and for the support of public credit." Also, the secretary was to report estimates of revenue and expenditures, establish accounts for warrants issued from the Treasury pursuant to appropriations by law, take charge of the sale of lands of the United States, and perform other services with respect to the finances.

The uniqueness of the Treasury in its relations with the houses of Congress has remained in considerable degree to the present time. The Treasury is still exceptional among the executive departments in its closeness to Congress.[32]

The Constitution prescribes methods of appointment but says nothing about removal of officers. The first session of Congress debated the matter at length. Eventually, it refuted the contention that officials appointed with consent of the Senate are not to be removed by a president without approval of the Senate. Madison argued strongly against that contention. His idea that the president should have sole removal authority may have reflected a belief that the Senate should not be a president's council. Nevertheless, the action of Congress was virtually constitutional in character. In the post–Civil War years, a hostile Congress enacted the Tenure of Office Act, which denied the president the sole removal authority. In 1926 the Supreme Court held that law contrary to the constitution. The Court treated the 1789 action of Congress as organic in character.[33]

The First Congress continued the Post Office, founded by preceding Congresses, on a temporary basis. Within a few years this was made permanent. The Post Office did not become a department until 1872, but the postmaster general became a member of the president's cabinet in 1829.[34]

The only new institution in the executive system at 1789 was the office of attorney general. This was authorized in the Judiciary Act of 1789. The attorney general acted as a cabinet member, but the Department of Justice was not established until 1870. The "downplaying" of the attorney general at 1789 may have been part of the general effort to soften the new coercive powers of the central government.

The growth of the department structure was slow at first and then came in spurts. The Navy became a separate department in

1798. The Department of Interior, with functions from both State and War Departments, was established in 1849. In two decades, 1870–89, Justice, the Post Office, and Agriculture were departmentalized. The Department of Commerce and Labor came into being in 1903 and became two departments in 1913. The military departments were united into the Department of Defense in 1947. The Army, Navy, and Air Force became subdepartments of Defense with separate secretaries for the three service departments.

Five new departments have been established since 1950. Health, Education and Welfare (HEW) was created in 1953 and Housing and Urban Development in 1965. The Department of Transportation was founded in 1966 and Energy in 1977. In 1978 HEW was divided into Health and Human Services in one department and Education in another. One department was eliminated when the Post Office became a government corporation in 1970.

About a century ago, Congress began establishing "independent agencies," that is, commissions, boards, or administrations, outside any department. Now there are many such entities, ranging in size and function. About 40 have substance and they vary greatly in number of employees. Government corporations, such as the Post Office, are included in this general group.

The institutionalization of the presidency began in 1939. The executive office of the president has an average of about ten agencies including the Office of Management and Budget.

The United States Government Manual 1983/1984 classifies the various units of the executive branch under three headings: executive office of the president; executive agencies and departments; and independent establishments and government corporations. Each area will be divided into two subgroups, according to its closeness to the presidency. Thus there are six classes:

Executive Office of the President
    1. White House Office
    2. The other executive office agencies
Executive Departments
    3. Inner group—State, Defense, Treasury, and Justice
    4. Outer group—the other departments
Independent Establishments and Government Corporations
    5. Management agencies
    6. Boards, commissions, corporations

These six classes are arranged in the above outline to show the general distance from the presidency. The larger the number, the farther the class of units is from the Oval Office. The farther away a unit is, the more likely that it is under the influence of Congress or its committees.

The "inner group" and "outer group" of departments are not unified groups. These terms have been used by analysts to indicate which department heads are closest to the president. Those of State, Defense, Treasury, and Justice are more likely to be consulted by the president, but the consultation is usually individual and not by group.[35]

This presentation is intended to indicate that the institutional presidency may be substantially separate from much of the executive branch.

PARTY COMPOSITION OF THE REPRESENTATIONAL BRANCH

The Constitutional Convention hoped that elections and operations would be free of political parties, but a two-party system in which the "probusiness" and the "proworker" oppose each other has existed during most of the 200 years of our constitutional life.

The names of the parties have changed somewhat. The "probusiness" party has been called Federalist, National Republican, Whig, and Republican, while the "proworker" was first named Republican and then Democratic. For more than a hundred years, the two parties have been consistently named Republican and Democratic. From 1860 to 1930 the Republican Party was generally in the majority, but since 1932 the Democratic has usually been in the majority. But throughout both periods there was a considerable amount of "divided government."

As indicated in the introduction, there are four general causes of party division or imbalance. First, the president is of one party and the majority of Congress of the other party. Second, the two houses of Congress have different majorities. Third, there is meaningful division within a majority party in Congress, such as the southern Democrats tending to agree with western Republicans. Fourth, there is some imbalance arising from the two-party organization of a house of Congress and the one-party domination of the presidency and the executive departments.

The situation of a president of one party and one or both houses of Congress having a majority of the other party has been called "divided government," even though there may be other forms of division. This has happened with 14 of the 42 Congresses during this century. In five of those instances, only one house had a majority of the nonpresidential party; that is, the two houses were divided.

The real political division within Congress has been on conservative/liberal grounds. There are a substantial number of southern Democrats who sided with the Republicans on many pieces of "liberal welfare" legislation. There is a division within the Republican Party, but it is not as large as the one in the Democratic Party. Democratic presidents have had strong support only three times in this century: Woodrow Wilson during 1913–14; Franklin Roosevelt during 1933–37, and Lyndon Johnson during 1964–67. In this last situation, President Johnson had adopted Kennedy's program, and he received support out of sympathy for Kennedy.

The imbalance caused by a one-party White House and a two-party Congress has not been the subject of much analysis. There is no official recognition of the approximately 40 percent who did not vote for the successful presidential candidate. That minority may appeal to the party in Congress, but those members have particular districts or states to represent. There is also the loss of the experience of those political executives who served a president who is no longer in the White House.

NOTES

1. William J. Keefe, *Congress and the American People* (Englewood Cliffs, N.J.: Prentice-Hall, 1980), p. 19.

2. John Helmer, "The Presidential Office: Velvet Fist in an Iron Glove," in Hugh Heclo and Lester M. Salamon, eds., *The Illusion of Presidential Government* (Boulder, Colo.: Westview Press, 1981), p. 65.

3. For analyses of the establishment of the new constitutional government in 1789, see Andrew C. McLaughlin, *A Constitutional History of the United States* (New York: Appleton-Century-Crofts, 1935), pp. 224–63; Arthur E. Sutherland, *Constitutionalism in America: Origin and Evolution of Fundamental Ideas* (New York: Blaisdell, 1965), pp. 184–89; Carl Brent Swisher, *American Constitutional Development* (Boston: Houghton Mifflin, 1943), pp. 45–63; H. von Holst, *The Constitutional and Political History of the United States* (Chicago: Callaghan, 1889), pp. 80–99; Alfred H. Kelly and Winfred A. Harbison, *The American Constitution: Its Origins and Development*, 4th ed. (New York: Norton, 1970), pp. 167–201.

4. Henry Steele Commager, ed., *Documents of American History,* 5th ed., vol. 1 (New York: Appleton-Century-Crofts, 1949), documents 38, 56, 61, 72, pp. 57, 82, 92, 111.

5. McLaughlin, *Constitutional History,* pp. 17-82. Edmund S. Morgan, *The Birth of the Republic, 1763-1789* (Chicago: University of Chicago Press, 1956), pp. 62-77.

6. Morgan, *Birth of the Republic,* pp. 113-28.

7. Wilfred E. Binkley, *President and Congress* (New York: Knopf, 1947), pp. 26-28; McLaughlin, *Constitutional History*, pp. 238-39.

8. Binkley, *President and Congress,* pp. 27-28, 33.

9. Ibid., p. 27.

10. Ibid.

11. Ibid., pp. 27-28.

12. Morgan, *Birth of the Republic,* pp. 124-25.

13. "In republican government, the legislative necessarily predominates." James Madison, *The Federalist Papers* (New York: New American Library, 1961), p. 322 (Letter no. 51).

14. "To put the Constitution into effect and the government into operation, the old Congress named the first Wednesday in January for the appointment of presidential electors, the first Wednesday in February for the election of the President, and the first Wednesday in March, which was the fourth day of the month, for the establishment of the new government at New York, then the meeting-place of Congress. The new legislature met with the deliberation characteristic of those days. A quorum of the House was not in attendance until the first of April and of the Senate not until some days later. Washington was declared elected President and Adams Vice-President; the President took the oath of office April 30, 1789. Even before the inauguration of the President the House had gone to work upon a revenue bill, which was passed after some weeks of discussion, and after modification by the Senate the act became a law; the new government had means of getting revenue. At an early date provision was made for the organization of executive departments." McLaughlin, *Constitutional History,* p. 224.

15. *The Public Statutes at Large of the United States of America,* vol. 1 (Boston: Little, Brown, 1854), pp. xvii-xxxii (List of Acts).

16. Ibid., pp. 264-65, 424-25.

17. Ibid., pp. 95-96.

18. Ibid., pp. 243-246.

19. Ibid., pp. 95, 119, 241, 264, 345, 367, 403, 424, 453-54.

20. Ibid., pp. 24-27.

21. Ibid., pp. 27, 29, 69, 112, 135, 145, 188, 219, 259, 274, 336, 373, 390, 411, 420, 476.

22. Ibid., pp. 55, 94, 106, 131, 229, 287, 305, 347, 369, 426, 444, 477, 489, 498, 516.

23. Ibid., pp. 112, 265, 302, 353, 369, 381, 497, 506.

24. Ibid., pp. 73-93; McLaughlin, *Constitutional History,* pp. 234-37; Sutherland, *Constitutionalism in America,* pp. 187-89; Swisher, *American Constitutional Development,* pp. 56-61; Kelly and Harbison, *American Constitution,* pp. 172-74.

25. Kelly and Harbison, *American Constitution,* pp. 484–85.

26. *Public Statutes at Large,* vol. 1, pp. 264–65.

27. Worthington C. Ford, *The Writings of George Washington,* vol. 12 (New York: G. P. Putnam's Sons, 1891).

28. Binkley, *President and Congress,* p. 27.

29. *Public Statutes at Large,* vol. 1, pp. 28, 49, 65, 68.

30. *Notes of Debates in the Federal Convention of 1787 Reported by James Madison* (New York: Norton, 1966), p. 389, August 6, 1787.

31. *Public Statutes at Large,* vol. 1, pp. 65–67.

32. Binkley, *President and Congress,* p. 31.

33. *Myers v. United States,* 272 U.S. 52 (1926); Kelly and Harbison, *American Constitution,* pp. 718–21.

34. For the data on the executive departments, see *The United States Governmental Manual* (Washington, D.C.: Government Printing Office, 1984).

35. Harold Seidman, *Politics, Position and Power: The Dynamics of Federal Organization* (New York: Oxford University Press, 1970), pp. 100–01; Thomas E. Cronin, *The State of the Presidency* (Boston: Little, Brown, 1975). "The inner cabinet, consisting of the departments of State, Defense, Treasury, and Justice, is more responsive to the President than the outer ring. They are less client-oriented departments; in fact, the President is their chief client." Erwin C. Hargrove, *The Power of the Modern Presidency* (Philadelphia: Temple University Press, 1974), pp. 238–39.

8

Changing Priorities of
Congressional Relationships

Congress is not organized to formulate a broad, consistent, national legislative program dealing with the problems of the time. Its authority is dispersed among numerous committees and subcommittees, each charged with considering legislation within a particular area. . . . Congress is best qualified to consider the legislation recommended by the President and the executive departments and by its own members.

Joseph P. Harris[1]

Congress responds to immediate demands. Members do not come to understand an economic crisis in abstract terms. They experience it in the form of demands from constituents and interest groups who seek relief from the problems caused by the crisis.

Philip Brenner[2]

The major check on presidential power, then, may well be not Congress in its legislative capacity, but Congress in its executive capacity allied with the bureaucracy and special interest groups.

Philippa Strum[3]

The House of Representatives established its legislative and representative primacy as soon as the Constitution began to operate in 1789. In fact, it was the center of policy activity for several years. The preceding chapter examined the extent of the statutory enactment in even the first and second year. The House benefited, of

103

course, from the ideas and the activity of Alexander Hamilton. The way in which that executive official brought action and unity to the Congress has relevance to the problem of presidential-congressional relationships even today.

Diversity within the House increased as years passed.[4] An act of Congress in 1842 required U.S. representatives to be elected by single-member districts. Likewise, members of both houses seemed to respond more and more to particular interests. The greater diversity means increased need for presidential guidance if there is to be more group coordination in the making of high-level policy.

This chapter will discuss the changing priorities within Congress. The next chapter will explain the changing priorities of the presidency, and then Chapters 10 and 11 will examine certain shared responsibilities of Congress and the presidency.

THE INCREASING INSTITUTIONAL DIVERSITY

The attitudes of Congress toward the presidency are much affected by the developments in the organizational structure of the houses of Congress, individually and collectively.[5] Legislative assemblies are by nature loosely organized, and this is accentuated in the U.S. system.[6] We developed during the colonial period a deep desire for area representation as opposed to the "common" or national unit representation in the British system.[7]

Our historical belief in the primacy and superiority of Congress derives also from the guiding role of Congresses in our national independence and our constitutional founding.[8] There is much that is not efficient or even effective in representative/legislative assemblies, and we may condemn them but we will not part with them.

The history of the operating structure of Congress is further evidence of the flexibility of the constitutional system. During the course of nearly 200 years, there has been a considerable series of inner mechanisms that have been dominant in influence at one time or another. Examples are the procedural devices of the Committee of the Whole, the select or temporary committee, the specialized standing committee, the presiding officer, the party leaders, the policy committee, the party caucus, the rules committee, the investigating committee, the appropriation committee, the budget committee, the joint committee, the "bipartisan" committee, and so on.[9]

When the Congress under the 1787 Constitution began to operate, it had available precedents from the British House of Commons, the state legislative bodies, and the Congress under the Articles of Confederation.

Parliamentary procedure may have been more important in the House of Representatives than in the Senate because of the larger numbers.[10] At the start the dominant device was the Committee of the Whole House.[11] It was favored by some state legislatures and was used during the first two weeks of the Constitutional Convention. The requirement for a quorum was small, and the rules of debate and action were comparatively flexible.

When the discussion of a proposed bill had developed a consensus, the practice in the House was to assign the drafting to a select committee. There was such a committee for each bill, and during the Third Congress there were 350 select, or temporary, one-bill committees.[12] Apparently, there was already need for reform.

Two added features raised the efficiency during the first quarter century. One pertained to only the Washington and Jefferson administrations, while the other was a permanent, continuing development. The first was the exceptional assistance given Congress by the secretaries of the treasury: Alexander Hamilton in the early Washington years and Albert Gallatin in the Jeffersonian era. Hamilton's role is much better known. He was a person of unusual energy and acumen, but Gallatin was equally brilliant in financial matters, and he had served in the House of Representatives.[13]

Standing committees were slow in coming. The first two in the House concerned elections and enrolled bills.[14] Specialized subject committees started in five years, but by 1820 there were only 15. Most standing committees in the Senate began in 1816.[15]

The emergence of two political parties during the 1790s had considerable effect upon the organization and operation of the houses of Congress and their relationships with the president. This was in addition to the effect of the parties upon nomination and election of the president. During the 12 years of the Washington and Adams terms, the Federalist Party was seldom a strong unifying force. In fact, it may have caused dissension in the Adams cabinet.

Jefferson brought close party relationships between Congress and the president, but Jefferson was a unique president in this regard.[16] For most of the nineteenth century, there was recurrent conflict between Congress and the president.[17] There were only a few presidents with the strength or skill to dominate the houses of Congress. Mostly, there was conflict or drift. Jackson, Polk, Lincoln, Hayes, Cleveland, and McKinley were the best, and often their influence was more negative than positive. At different periods, the Senate was dominant, and at other periods there was more drift than domination.

The political parties were not strong. At least a third of the time after 1840, the president and Congress were divided in terms of party. The average tenure of the presidents was less than four years. From 1876 to 1892 five consecutive presidents were elected with less than 50 percent of the popular vote. Yet important legislation, such as Civil Service, the Interstate Commerce Commission, and the Anti-Trust Act, was enacted.

A number of events since 1900 have tended to increase still more the decentralization of Congress, and particularly the House of Representatives:

The reduction of the strong powers of the Speaker of the House in 1910.

The resulting increase in the authority and power of the chairmen of specialized committees.

The establishment of the Bureau of the Budget in 1921. This began the domination of the general budgetary process by the institutionalized presidency.

The establishment of the General Accounting Office in 1921, which provides the specialized committees of Congress with information about executive departments and agencies. The investigative activity of the committees was aided also by the Supreme Court decision in 1927 upholding such activity.

The increased pressures by special interest groups and the increased legislation in regulatory and development activity. This is evident also in the new departments for health, education, welfare, transportation, education, urban development, and housing and in new comparable committees.

The lack of permanent success of congressional reorganizations and other efforts to reduce the number of committees.

The considerable increase in the number of subcommittees and the shift of authority and power from committee chairmen to subcommittee chairmen. In the Senate almost every member of the majority party is a chairman. There are more than 100 subcommittees in the House of Representatives.

The increased attention that members of Congress pay to their particular constituencies.

The tendency of both voters and representatives to turn away from political party identification and the unifying power of central party organization.[18]

The total effect of these developments is evident in this 1977 analysis of congressional structure and operation:

> Not only has the number of subcommittees undergone a drastic increase, but their powers and autonomy also have increased in the wake of changes (called "reforms," of course) that occurred in the House in the early 1970s. First, in 1971 members were limited to the chairmanship of one subcommittee. Senior members who were hoarding chairmanships were forced to relinquish them to less senior members. . . . it is clear that the twenty-odd full committee chairmen have been weakened and the 120-odd subcommittee chairmen strengthened. Congress now has a surfeit of chiefs and a shortage of Indians.[19]

The fragmentation of Congress is evident also in the "lobbying" tactics used by presidents to gain program victories in Congress. Several major proposals by President Reagan apparently were doomed until he resorted to wholesale "lobbyist" methods. He used person-to-person blandishments that either flattered members of Congress or raised their hopes of future support. They threw their backing to the White House and allowed the president to win highly important last-minute victories.

CONGRESSIONAL DISPERSION OF THE LEGISLATIVE FUNCTIONS

The meaning of *legislative power* is neither clear nor consistent. Sometimes it stands for the congressional institution and other times for the making of statutes, and still other times for different things. The Supreme Court might be expected to be consistent because it has a sense of identity with the past and the future. But in the course of two centuries it had raised as well as answered questions.

An 1800 opinion by Justice William Patterson, who had been the leading New Jersey delegate at the 1787 convention, set forth an inclusive definition of legislative power. He may have had state legislatures in mind when he said that "wherever the legislative power of a government is undefined, it includes the judicial and executive attributes."[20] Alexander Hamilton had defined executive power in that way. Contemporary welfare liberals tend to define presidential power in such a manner.

Chief Justice John Marshall suggested simple agreement of institution and function in a noted 1810 opinion when he stated that "to the legislature all legislative power is granted."[21] But, in the particular case, the Supreme Court held that the Georgia legislature had contracted and not legislated when it had granted tracts of land a few years previously. That finding allowed the Court to decide that the contract provision of the national constitution prohibited Georgia from rescinding the grants even though they may have been tainted with fraud. But Marshall said that there is no clear answer to "how far the power of giving the law may involve every other power when the Constitution is silent on the matter."[22]

The start of Article I of the Constitution may vest legislative powers in Congress, but Capitol Hill has increasingly shared the process of making law with the judiciary, the presidency, the political executives of the specialized departments, and the career civil servants of the vast administrative bureaucracy.

Congressional delegation began early. The Judiciary Act of 1789, and an additional act of 1793, empowered the courts to regulate their practice. The Supreme Court issued such regulations, and their validity was considered by the Supreme Court in an 1825 opinion. The Court refuted the contention that Congress had exceeded its authority in authorizing the judiciary to make rules that Congress itself could have made.[23]

The 1825 opinion of Chief Justice John Marshall touched both poles. It affirmed the vesting formula of the Constitution that, in Marshall's words, "the legislative makes, the executive executes, and the judiciary construes the law."[24] The chief justice preserved the theory of legislative sovereignty in Congress by declaring that Congress must keep to itself "powers which are strictly and exclusively legislative."[25]

The Court did not identify those exclusive powers and seems never to have done so specifically. Probably, it would include, if not be limited to, penal legislation. But, with the exception of the unidentified sacred area, Congress may delegate to other government institutions, "powers which the legislature may rightfully exercise itself."[26]

The chief justice did not attempt to mark out the boundary and in fact acknowledged its uncertainty: "The line has not been exactly drawn which separates those important subjects, which must be entirely regulated by the legislature itself, from those of less interest, in which a general provision may be made, and power given to those who are to act under such general provisions to fill up the details."[27]

That particular case involved a delegation to the courts, but the formula of having other institutions "fill up the details" has been applied to other types of delegations, and in many instances the details have had considerable substance. For instance, in 1892 the Supreme Court held proper a congressional grant to the president to revise a schedule of import duties, even while asserting that "Congress cannot delegate legislative power to the President."[28]

There has been a vast amount of delegation to executive units. In the 1930s the Supreme Court disapproved of New Deal delegations of industry code-making authority to private associations.[29] But the Court has not held invalid delegation to an official government agency. It even approved in 1947 a statute without explicit standards for the regulation of investment banking and in 1950 and 1965 upheld delegations that may have abridged the rights of individuals to exit visas.[30]

There may be a limitation on congressional delegation to administrative agencies that has not been tested directly and definitely. When Congress has given a regulatory agency the power to issue subpoenas, it has placed final enforcement authority in the courts. There has been a dictum that judicial finality is a constitutional requirement. That was indicated in a 1894 Supreme Court opinion.[31]

Scholarly observations of the national administration, and particularly of congressional-presidential relationships, have called attention to the extent to which Congress has directly or indirectly delegated legislative-like authority to executive departments and agencies:

> Laws are also frequently passed in largely skeletal form conferring considerable discretionary powers on administrators. . . . Thus, the bureaucracy must frequently make choices and decisions that are, in effect, policy making.[32]

> By defining "the public interest" in broad nebulous terms, Congress is allowing policy to be made by administrators on the basis of the inputs from constituencies of administrative agencies.[33]

Policy-making on issues not receiving wide national policy is often accomplished through interaction of Congressional and bureaucratic specialists and the representatives of the concerned constituencies.[34]

Other analysts of congressional-executive interactions make similar statements about the extent to which Congress makes substantial delegations to institutions in the executive and judicial systems.[35]

Congress during recent decades has developed a way of dealing with the executive units that may be more efficient than constitutional. This combines broad delegation of authority with the reservation of a "legislative veto" if the executive use of the authority does not satisfy the houses of Congress or, in some instances, either one of them. The Supreme Court in 1983 held a one-house veto unconstitutional because there was no bicameral action and no presentment to the president.[36]

The Court action may have upset many such arrangements. There may, however, be other ways of gaining the same result. Louis Fisher, probably the foremost scholarly analyst on these matters, points out that Congress can grant powers for short periods and, when the president asks for reenactment, either house could prevent the extension by opposing the new legislation. Fisher observes in a 1985 study that such cooperation will be arrived at in some way:

> With or without the legislative veto, Congress will remain a partner in "shared administration." It is inconceivable that any court or any President can prevent it. Call it supervision, intervention, interference, or just plain meddling, Congress will find a way. And government is not the worse off for it.[37]

Thus legislation is not simply an enactment by Congress and an application by the executive. It is a continuing process of grant and use and adjustment. This is more evidence that separate functions have become a fusion or exchange of mutual efforts.

THE INCREASING DIVERSITY OF CONGRESSIONAL FUNCTIONS

With the dispersion of the legislative functions among other institutions, Congress has developed a multiplicity of other functions. The sheer diversity of its action is portrayed quite sharply by John S. Saloma III, of the Massachusetts Institute of Technology, in his analysis of Congress. He identifies 11 specific functions and 7 general ones:

I. *Specific Functions*
    A. Major
        1. Representative (articulation, aggregation, and communication of constituency demands or interests).
        2. Legislative (passage of laws, resolutions, etc., in constitutionally specified fields, especially revenue and appropriation).
        3. Control of administration (oversight or review of administration of legislation, appropriations, and investigation).
        4. Investigative (research into basic social and economic problems, probable consequences of legislation, and evaluation of existing programs).
        5. Informative (informing and educating the public and communicating information to constituents).
        6. Constituent service (answering constituent requests and servicing specific constituent interests).
    B. Other
        1. Judicial (impeachment and judging elections, returns, and qualification of members).
        2. Executive counsel (making treaties and confirming appointments).
        3. Constituent (developing amendments to the Constitution).
        4. Leadership (electing president when the electoral college fails to produce a majority, determining the order of presidential succession).
        5. Internal organization (determining own rules and procedures).
II. *General Functions*
        1. Conflict management (adjustment of interest demands through bargaining and compromise).
        2. Integration (relating popular policies to governmental performance).
        3. Legitimation (ratification of governmental decisions through constitutional procedure, delegation of

authority to other governmental agents).

4. Participation (affording multiple access to decision making, maximizing opportunities for expressing interest and public review).

5. Recruitment and development of political leadership (for higher elected positions including the presidency).

6. Education of a democratic electorate (clarifying policy, identifying and publicizing issues, and forming opinions).

7. Adaptation (responding to changed requirements for a government that facilitates changes in the political system).[38]

The function not expressly prescribed by the Constitution that comes nearest to being a rival to legislation is investigation, usually by a committee or subcommittee.

The first investigation by a house of Congress of an executive activity was in 1791.[39] It sought to find the reason for a military defeat at the hands of Indians. In 1857 Congress passed a statute that made refusal to testify before a congressional body a misdemeanor. The Supreme Court limited investigations in 1881 but upheld them in 1927.[40] This last opinion said that investigations were incidental to the legislative process. Committee hearings reached new heights in the post-1950 period because of the aid of television. An analysis and assessment of the function appears in Joseph P. Harris's *Congress and the Legislative Process:*

> The conduct of investigations has become a major function of Congress, often overshadowing in public attention its legislative activities. Congressional investigations serve several purposes: (1) They provide much of the information that is needed to enact legislation. (2) They enable Congress through its committees to check on the administration of the programs that it has authorized and to hold executive officers responsible. (3) They inform and educate the public and influence public opinion. Congressional investigations cover a very wide range of subjects. The largest number deal with the administration of the executive departments and agencies.[41]

The growth of the investigative function has altered basically the relations of Congress with the executive institutions and that in turn affects relations with the president.

THE HIGH POLICY FUNCTIONS OF CONGRESS

With the increasing decentralization of structure and the spread of functions, described in the preceding sections, the houses of Congress encounter increased difficulties. Their constituents demand more attention, and that enlarges the task of reaching a common answer to high policy issues. As a result, there is greater need for the unifying activism of the president.

These developments are compounded by the larger role of the houses of Congress and their extensive committee systems in setting policies for the organization and operation of the executive departments and agencies. Scholarly analysts attest to the upper-level responsibility of Congress in this area:

> The "organic power," which is the power to create and abolish agencies, is entirely contained in Congress. There is no way in which this authority can be inferred from Article II [the presidential article].[42]

> The mission and structure of the departments are determined by Act of Congress.[43]

> Congress has a legitimate role and responsibility in supervising the efforts of the federal agencies. . . . Agencies have a direct responsibility to Congress which created them.[44]

Much of the middle-level operation of the national government is directed by the committees, working in conjunction with the corresponding executive institutions. Here there is more evidence of the common responsibilities of the three elected institutions. Also, the upper-level officials of the executive and legislative departments may concentrate upon the high-level policies.

The judiciary has been most supportive of the president and the executive when they endeavor to execute legislation by Congress. For instance, in 1867 the Supreme Court refused to enjoin President Andrew Johnson from enforcing the post–Civil War Reconstruction Acts adopted by Congress. The Court said it would not restrain in advance the execution of an act of Congress on grounds of unconstitutionality. Later, it made a similar holding in a suit against the secretary of war, the official immediately concerned with application of the statutes.[45]

In those cases, Congress acted first. Chapter 11 will examine situations in which the presidents acted before congressional authorization.

The changing priorities of Congress have involved increased demands for legislation and greater difficulty in legislating. Much of the trouble arises from the decentralization and even disunity of the houses of Congress, which has meant an increased dependence upon the initiative and unifying activism of the president. The next chapter will show that the changing priorities of the presidency may allow more time and aid for the legislative program. Thus there is room for more cooperation and increased development of the group character of the three elected institutions.

NOTES

1. Joseph P. Harris, *Congress and the Legislative Process*, 2d ed. (New York: McGraw-Hill, 1972), pp. 162–63.

2. Philip Brenner, "An Approach to the Limits and Possibilities of Congress," in Lawrence C. Dodd and Bruce L. Oppenheimer, eds., *Congress Reconsidered*, 2d ed. (Washington, D.C.: Congressional Quarterly Press, 1981), p. 382.

3. Philippa Strum, *Presidential Power and American Democracy*, 2d ed. (Santa Monica, Calif.: Goodyear Publishing, 1979), p. 88.

4. "Members of Congress are inevitably caught in a crossfire of competing expectations. They are national legislators, charged with such exalted goals as furthering the national interest, providing for the common defense, and promoting the general welfare. They are also local representatives, elected by and accountable to narrow geographic constituencies, and held responsible for protecting and advancing myriad local interests. Most policy debates in Congress reflect both forces." R. Douglas Arnold, "The Local Roots of Domestic Policy," in Thomas E. Mann and Norman J. Ornstein, eds., *The New Congress* (Washington, D.C.: American Enterprise Institute, 1981), p. 250.

5. William F. Mullen, *Presidential Power and Politics* (New York: St. Martin's Press, 1976), pp. 6–7; C. Herman Pritchett, "The President's Constitutional Position," in Thomas E. Cronin, ed., *Rethinking the Presidency* (Boston: Little, Brown, 1982), pp. 127–38.

6. "The president's nature is unity; that of Congress, diversity." Charles M. Hardin, *Presidential Power and Accountability* (Chicago: University of Chicago Press, 1974), p. 14. "Congress represents the rich diversity of American life, the President its necessary unity." Louis W. Koenig, *The Chief Executive*, 4th ed. (New York: Harcourt Brace Jovanovich, 1981), p. 157.

7. "Declaration and Resolves of the First Continental Congress," pars. 4 and 10, in Henry S. Commager, ed., *Documents of American History*, 5th ed., vol. 1 (New York: Appleton-Century-Crofts, 1949), pp. 82–84.

8. The independent founding of the United States was directed by a series of Congresses, the Stamp Act Congress, the First and Second Continental Congresses, and the Congress of the Confederation. Edmund S. Morgan, *The Birth of the Republic: 1763-1789* (Chicago: University of Chicago Press, 1956), pp. 24-25, 61-77, 101-28.

9. "The Committees of Congress," "Committee Activities," and "Power Structure of Congress," in George B. Galloway, *The Legislative Process in Congress* (New York: Crowell, 1953), pp. 273-353.

10. "A member of the House of Representatives is a private in the ranks. . . . Each Senator, on the other hand, is a staff officer—even a prima donna." Charles O. Jones, *The United States Congress* (Homewood, Ill.: Dorsey Press, 1982), p. 265, quoting Lindsay Rogers, *The American Senate* (New York: Alfred Knopf, 1926), pp. 253-55.

11. *Origins and Development of Congress* (Washington, D.C.: Congressional Quarterly Press, 1982), p. 99; Wilfred E. Binkley, *President and Congress* (New York: Knopf, 1947), pp. 32-33.

12. Galloway, *Legislative Process*, p. 273.

13. Binkley, *President and Congress*, pp. 31-45, 54.

14. Galloway, *Legislative Process*, p. 274.

15. Ibid.

16. Binkley, *President and Congress*, pp. 54-65; Alfred H. Kelly and Winfred A. Harbison, *The American Constitution: Its Origins and Development*, 4th ed. (New York: Norton, 1970), pp. 224-61; Commager, *Documents of American History*, vol. 1, pp. 211-12.

17. Binkley, *President and Congress*, pp. 66-85. "Even more than Washington, Jackson laid the foundations for the modern presidential office." Kelly and Harbison, *American Constitution*, pp. 335.

18. *Origins and Development of Congress*, pp. 129-84; Galloway, *Legislative Process*, pp. 327-69, 426-59, 591-626.

19. Morris P. Fiorina, *Congress: Keystone of the Washington Establishment* (New Haven: Yale University Press, 1977), pp. 64-66. \

20. *Cooper v. Telfair*, 4 Dallas 14, 15-16, 19 (1800).

21. *Fletcher v. Peck*, 6 Cranch 87 (1810).

22. Ibid., p. 136.

23. *Wayman v. Southard*, 10 Wheaton 1 (1825).

24. Ibid., p. 46.

25. Ibid., pp. 42-43.

26. Ibid.

27. Ibid.

28. *Field v. Clark*, 143 U.S. 649, 692 (1892).

29. *Schechter v. U.S.*, 295 U.S. 495 (1935); *Panama Refining Co. v. Ryan*, 293 U.S. 388 (1935).

30. *Fahey v. Mallonee*, 332 U.S. 245 (1947); *Knauff v. Shaughnessy*, 338 U.S. 537 (1950); *Zemel v. Rusk*, 381 U.S. 1 (1965).

31. There may be dicta to that effect in *Interstate Commerce Commission v. Brimson*, 154 U.S. 447 (1894). That case approved the use of the contempt power of the courts to aid the enforcement of orders of the Commission.

32. Dale Vinyard, *The Presidency* (New York: Scribner's, 1971), p. 117.

33. Peter Woll, *Public Policy* (Cambridge, Mass.: Winthrop, 1974), p. 9.

34. Gary Orfield, *Congressional Power: Congress and Social Change* (New York: Harcourt Brace Jovanovich, 1975), p. 83.

35. C. Herman Pritchett, *The American Constitutional System* (New York: McGraw-Hill, 1981), p. 33; Louis Fisher, *President and Congress: Power and Policy* (New York: Free Press, 1972), p. 57; Joseph P. Harris, *Congress and the Legislative Process* (New York: McGraw-Hill, 1972), pp. 5–6.

36. *Immigration and Naturalization Service v. Chadha,* 103 S. Ct. 2764 (1983).

37. Louis Fisher, *Constitutional Conflicts between Congress and the President* (Princeton: Princeton University Press, 1985), p. 183.

38. John S. Saloma III, *Congress and the New Politics* (Boston: Little, Brown, 1969), pp. 22–23.

39. Binkley, *President and Congress,* p. 40.

40. *Kilbourn v. Thompson,* 103 U.S. 168 (1881); *McGrain v. Daugherty,* 273 U.S. 135, 177, 178 (1927).

41. Harris, *Congress and the Legislative Process,* p. 166.

42. Woll, *Public Policy,* p. 29.

43. Koenig, *Chief Executive,* p. 186.

44. Louis Fisher, *The Politics of Shared Powers: Congress and the Executive* (Washington, D.C.: Congressional Quarterly Press, 1981), p. 74.

45. *Mississippi v. Johnson,* 71 U.S. 475, 500 (1867); *Georgia v. Stanton,* 6 Wall. 50 (1868).

9

Changing Priorities of Presidential Relationships

> The rise of presidential authority cannot be accounted for by the intention of presidents: it is the product of political conditions which dominate all the departments of governement, so that Congress itself shows an unconscious disposition to aggrandize the presidential office.
>
> Henry Jones Ford[1]

> Although the presidency is the main center of political leadership in the American polyarchy, it is less the result of a carefully thought out design than of the continued growth of an institution very loosely prescribed by the Constitution.
>
> Robert A. Dahl[2]

> Where can one find a finer example of the natural history of our political institutions than the way in which the dynamic forces of American society have transformed the chief executive of the written Constitution into the chief legislator of our unwritten constitution.
>
> Wilfred Binkley[3]

The preceding chapter on the changing priorities of the Houses of Congress addressed developments in the presidency during our nearly 200 years under the Constitution of 1787. In fact, Congress has been a principal cause of the transformation of the executive presidency of the constitutional facade into the elevated presidency of the adapt-

117

ed Constitution, that is, from the presidency that follows Congress to the presidency that endeavors to lead and guide congressional formulation of public policy.

This chapter will carry forward the analyses of the adaptation of our constitutional system. It will elaborate on the efforts of presidents to direct the integration of public policy conflicts in the houses of Congress, and through them to coordinate the competitive forces of the administrative institutions and of the national society itself. The explanations in this chapter will lead to the next two chapters on the shared responsibilities of the three elected institutions with respect to both the legislative and the legitimative systems. They will deal with the major contemporary problem of how a slow-acting Congress can guide and channel a fast-acting president.

THE CONCEPT OF COORDINATIVE POLITICS

The term *politics* is one of the principal sources of difficulty in explaining—and understanding—the complexity of governmental relationships. Like many key words in our common language, politics has several meanings.[4] Two persons may assume different ideas about its signification even in the same conversation. They may think that they are communicating with each other when in fact neither may realize that they intend different concepts.

The range of meanings extends from a narrow, negative one to a broad, positive one. Many persons consider "politics" to be a self-centered, manipulative activity for getting and keeping a public office with little thought of the "public interest." The other polar meaning is that "politics" is a process of "conflict resolution," that is, of developing an accommodation between contrary positions such as those with respect to abortion.

Many scholarly analysts insist that "politics" is a necessary and positive element of government.[5] But those persons who take a negative view of "politics" and use it as a synonym for "bad" will hardly understand a professor who deems politics beneficial and necessary. They may conclude that the professor thinks we need to be bad.

We may be faced with a situation where informative communication is not possible. Neither side is likely to change its definition of politics, and an added difficulty is that seeking office and the integration of public conflicts often go hand in hand. Getting elected is often a matter of bringing conflicting forces in common support of the same program. The self-interest of being reelected may cause an incumbent to develop a position of accommodation between contrary groups of voters. The person elected may have the superior capacity for resolving conflicts, and that may well be in the public interest. Getting into office and performing the duties of the office may require similar attitudes and talents.

Despite the difficulties, we will endeavor to explain the concept of coordinative politics. A number of commentators assert that the conflict resolution concept of politics arises from the competitive or combative character of the national society:

> Individuality is the source of politics. Politics is a means of coping with the conflicts that human differences produce. . . . politics refers to all human efforts to resolve conflicts nonviolently by constructing laws or controls. . . .[6]

> The art of politics remains the art of reconciling power relationships to the needs of a society.[7]

> Politics implies a diversity of goals and values that must be reconciled before a decision can be reached.[8]

The difficulties of reconciling conflicts may increase when those who hold particular beliefs or desires are organized. The tendency of persons with common interests to organize is long-standing, but it has increased markedly during recent decades.

The whole complex set of relationships among organized groups and the public institutions has expanded the study of government into the study of the "political system." Its larger dimensions are evident in these two typical definitions:

> The political system includes the Congress, the President, the Court, and the bureaucracy: it also includes organized interest groups, political parties, and individuals as voters and expressors of opinion.[9]

> The political system of the United States institutionalizes a variety of values, some of them at odds with each other. . . . To ask what is to become of the presidency is to ask what is to become of the entire American political order.[10]

The fact that government functions within an outreaching political system may be a basic reason for the essential difference between a private business organization and a public governmental institution:

> A political process cannot be managed in the sense that a corporation is managed, for political decisions are judged according to their fairness, both in the way they are made and in their perceived effect.[11]

The assumption of many analysts that "politics" pertains to conflict resolution across the whole panorama of public and governmental relationships leads naturally to the firm idea that the activity of presidents in all of its variety is essentially and even necessarily political in character. This has been asserted by a number of specialists on the presidency:

> The strong president also recognizes that his vision cannot be achieved without deft manipulation of the existing political machinery.[12]

> We need expert politicians in the Presidency more than ever. It is only through politics that a democratic nation can be governed.[13]

> A President's first allegiance cannot be to his private conscience but to the public political system of which he is a part. Maintaining the legitimacy of that system must take precedence.[14]

Other specialists on the presidency emphasize the need of political skill in relations with other governmental institutions:

> An effective president is an effective politician. Although the public may often say it wants the president to be above politics, the job nevertheless requires him to be a political mobilizer, a salesman for his program, a lobbyist and a politician in chief. We have so designed our system with checks and balances and dispersed powers that no change is possible without a skilled coalition builder in the White House.[15]

The views of the commentators above indicate definitely that "politics" is important to performance; it cannot be left behind when a president enters the White House. In the following statement, Morrow assesses the concept beneath the broad meaning of politics.

Politics can be defined as a struggle among competing forces for the right to control the character of public policy. The key component in this definition is the term *struggle*. The notion of a struggle implies that competitors have different objectives in mind and that each does battle with other competitors who seek different objectives.

Viewed in such a way, politics is virtually universal. It is found not only in government, but within churches, universities and families. On a higher plane it occurs between and among churches, universities, and within families.[16]

Political skill is not confined to some of the areas or levels of the presidency. It enters into all levels of presidential activity, from the execution of laws, through administration, legislation, representation, high policy coordination, and communication, to personification of the nation at the top. The roles of a president as chief of state in the rituals of democracy and sovereignty have their political aspects. A president's choice of events for "ceremonial" observance can affect his standing among certain groups in the variety of public interests. What he says at the most widely recognized holidays may bear upon his popularity with the members of Congress and the voters in various sections of the nation.[17]

THE CONTEMPORARY ESTEEM OF POSITIVE ACTIVISM

The scholarly analysis of presidential behavior during the past 50 years has often emphasized psychological and sociological factors more than law, history, and economics. Harold D. Lasswell suggested a connection between psychopathology and politics and between power and personality.[18] Erwin C. Hargrove asserted that personal insecurity and political skill were linked.[19] In 1960 Richard Neustadt argued that the power of the presidency is not the authority to command but the ability to persuade.[20]

These theories and explanations may have been attempts to understand the combination of success and failure in Theodore Roosevelt, Woodrow Wilson, and Franklin Roosevelt. Professors of history, government, and sociology generally class these three as the "great" presidents of this century, but each seemed to carry a good thing too far. The first Roosevelt tore his party apart in 1912, Wilson was morally rigid in the fight for the League of Nations, and the second Roosevelt used his great victory in 1936 to try to pack the Supreme Court for opposing some aspects of the New Deal.[21]

The constitutional politics in this development seems to have been that Congress was institutionally superior but weak in will-power, while the presidency was institutionally weak but capable of great strength when occupied by a person of dominant will and superior skill. According to Professor Hargrove, all presidents must be legislative leaders because Congress is not organized to lead.[22] Many academic commentators admire welfare activists apparently without regard to the psychology of insecurity. Dorothy James in her *The Contemporary Presidency* sets the following standard: "Most Americans judge their Presidents on the basis of their successful use of power to further the goal of creating a society within which the greatest possible degree of individual growth and development is possible."[23] Philippa Strum may have much the same idea when she says that Nixon fought for his position but not his *power* because he did not comprehend the use of the power to do something about the internal problems faced by the nation.[24]

Moral purpose may be the underlying quality that led James MacGregor Burns to distinguish management and leadership. In his 1978 volume *Leadership*, this is the difference between transactional and transformational leadership.[25] Douglas Yates makes a similar contrast with the terms *manager* and *moralist,* for Herbert Hoover and Woodrow Wilson, respectively.[26]

The most widely accepted classifications seem to be those that differentiate activity and inactivity. Professor Hargrove's *Presidential Leadership* starts with a simple, polar contrast between presidents of action and presidents of restraint.[27] Theodore Roosevelt, Woodrow Wilson, and Franklin Roosevelt are in the first group, and William Howard Taft, Herbert Hoover, and Dwight Eisenhower in the second.[28]

The best known classification of White House behavior is in James D. Barber's *Presidential Character,* which suggests that types of behavior may be predicted by analyzing kinds of personality.[29] Professor Barber foretold unhappy events for President Nixon. His system presents four types of presidential character. The classification combines an activity/passivity contrast and a positive/negative differentiation and presents four kinds of behavior: active-positive, active-negative, passive-positive, and passive-negative.[30] Barber illustrates the system by classifying 15 presidents:

Active-positive: Thomas Jefferson, Franklin Roosevelt, Harry Truman, and John F. Kennedy.

Active-negative: John Adams, Woodrow Wilson, Herbert Hoover, Lyndon Johnson, and Richard Nixon.

Passive-positive: James Madison, William H. Taft, and Warren G. Harding.

Passive-negative: George Washington, Calvin Coolidge, and Dwight Eisenhower.[31]

This may be the best simple categorization of presidents available, but we need to consider the merits of simple classification itself. The use of one set of polar contrasts to modify another twofold set may lessen extremism, but the whole approach seems to look upon the presidents as separated figures with little consideration of the public policy leadership needed to unite the conflicting elements in both the voting public and the houses of Congress.

THE DECLINE IN ADMINISTRATIVE RELATIONS

There has been, of course, considerable change in the aims and actions of the presidency during the long life of the Constitution. The most meaningful pattern for explaining the change is probably three types of relationships: administrative, congressional, and public. Congressional relationships may be the most relevant in considering the separate group character of the three elected institutions.

If we start with the introductory idea of the Constitution that the president is the executive power, then the primary development has been the decline in administrative relations. This is the consensus among several scholarly analysts.

The first proposition is that the president has a wide choice in the matter. This is recognized by Berkeley Professor Nelson W. Polsby, in his 1976 analysis *Congress and the Presidency.* He states that the president

is free to pursue those policies that are of greatest concern to him; he is not required to give equal attention to all problems and all agencies. Hence, it can be expected that most agencies most of the time will conduct their business according to the same pattern no matter who is President. But when a President desires to do so, he can change a particular agency's policies—if he is willing to bear the costs in terms of time, energy and perhaps also the enmity of bureaucrats and the interest groups who are served by the agency involved.[32]

The president's choice may reflect, at least to some degree, the demands upon the White House. Observations on this point include that of John Emmet Hughes, who served in the Eisenhower regime. He calls attention to "the eager readiness of Americans to believe in each new President's goodness and wiseness." Hughes asserts that there is a common belief that any president is "both the robed incarnation of the past and the armored prophet of the future." He concludes that "the full of such popular fantasies can press upon a President impossible demands."[33] Other specialists on the presidency make similar comments:

> Everybody now expects the man inside the White House to do something about everything.[34]

> Expectations about what a president is able to achieve are vastly inflated. The people now tend to hold the chief executive responsible for most of the difficulties that beset the body politic.[35]

> Americans vastly overrate the President's power—and they are likely to continue to do so.[36]

Chapter 6 explained that the demands of the public are more likely to concern legislation than execution. As a consequence there has been considerable decline in the administrative relations of a president.

Another factor that causes presidents to limit their administrative relations is the growing proposition that they can be more effective if they concentrate upon a few issues. President Reagan emphasized this strongly in setting himself apart from his predecessor who had overburdened Congress as well as himself in too large an agenda.

The wisdom of presidents in concentrating upon a few issues may result in many operating decisions being made by "lesser officials." This is the conclusion in two of the more profound analyses of government during the last half century:

There is in fact a real limit on the agencies to which the president can give thought. . . . the president . . . must maintain some of the detachment of a constitutional ruler. . . . Hence, as part of the price of effective presidential leadership, lesser officials must be held accountable for particular policies.[37]

The president's necessary detachment from numerous issues of administrative policy inevitably imposes a large measure of independence upon department heads, whether or not they are personally attached to his policies.[38]

These views reinforce the notion that the U.S. government, even within the single branch that is supposed to be a hierarchical pyramid with the president at the top, is actually a conglomeration, with many fairly autonomous centers of power.

This need not mean that presidents have no impact upon operations and policy making. It means that the person in the Oval Office exerts his influence at a higher level and on a wider field of endeavor. It may allow the president to be a larger and higher force with the public policy superstructure composed of the three elected institutions. He has more opportunity to meet the responsibilities of the chief representative and the national personality. These qualities are important in his efforts to lead the legislative efforts of the houses of Congress. There may also be the opportunity to exert influence upon specialized committees of Congress, and, indirectly, to exert added pressure upon another set of channels to the decision-making administrators in the specialized departments and agencies of the executive system.

The extralegal or informal relations of the president with the houses of Congress concern in large degree the preparation of proposed legislation. The analysis by George B. Galloway of the Legislative Reference Service during the 1950s indicates that there is a substantial amount of interplay between the three institutions.[39] Some more recent analysts have tried to show what percentage of enactments originated with members of Congress and what percentage with the president or an executive official. This may not be too meaningful since success is most likely to depend upon support from both ends of Pennsylvania Avenue. The need for common support is one of the conclusions drawn from Thomas E. Cronin's 1980 study *The State of the Presidency.*[40]

THE INCREASE IN PUBLIC RELATIONS

The continuing decline in the administrative relations of presidents may have allowed more time and effort for participation in the common functions of the representational group. There may be more opportunity to work with the houses of Congress in high-level policy making to guide the appointed officials in the legislative and executive systems.

Congressional relationships, however, have a rival and a very strong one. That is the deep and mutual interest of the president and the people in the public media. This is not entirely new. The use of newspapers to support public policy argument goes back to the first Washington term. Alexander Hamilton and James Madison, in their controversy over financial policies, each had the support of a gazette. One account is that the two gazettes set the precedent for government subsidizing partisan journalism by awarding printing contracts and giving patronage appointments.[41] Moreover, the use of the press continued. When Andrew Jackson was promoting his presidential candidacy, he founded a chain of hundreds of small town newspapers.

The twentieth century brought increased presidential skill in the promotional use of the established public media. Theodore Roosevelt was highly adroit in his relationships with newspapers, and Franklin Roosevelt gave a new dimension to the presidency with his radio "fireside chats" as well as his general skill.

Television, of course, has augmented the public projection of the presidents. John F. Kennedy made strategic use of that medium. His debate with Richard Nixon in 1960 was a victory, at least in the view of media commentators. Jimmy Carter was hailed as a great communicator during his first year in the White House, but his standing declined. In the 1980 debate he was surpassed by Ronald Reagan. As president, Reagan had extra skills. He was able to draw upon the public imagination more than any other president.

The public media, and perhaps the media public, have changed the character of nomination and election campaigns and even of the government. This is bound up with the decline of the two major parties. The extent to which sophisticated media affect the presidency is evident in the comments of scholarly analysts:

Media coverage is the lifeblood of politics because it shapes the political perceptions which form the reality on which political action is based.[42]

The American public has become conditioned by the media not to believe in the reality of a public act until it has been transformed into a dramatic or theatrical gesture before the camera. National personalities, including presidents, know they must try to acquire the attributes of show business.[43]

The dominance of the mass and elite media in U.S. public life has increased the importance of the presidential position in the minds of most citizens. The tendency of much of the public to assume that government is what the president says and does seems to raise a pertinent question. Are there two governments? In addition to the official, legal one, is there a public relations, media government with the president at its apex?

NOTES

1. Henry Jones Ford, *The Rise and Growth of American Politics* (New York: Macmillan, 1898), p. 284.
2. Robert A. Dahl, *Democracy in the United States,* 4th ed. (Chicago: Rand McNally, 1981), p. 69.
3. Wilfred E. Binkley, *The Man in the White House* (New York: Harper & Row, 1958), p. 132.
4. *"Politics.* Human activity concerned with making and implementing decisions vested with the authority of the society for which the decisions are made. No single phrase can capture the many meanings assigned to the word." Jack C. Plano and Robert E. Riggs, *Dictionary of Political Analysis* (Hindsdale, Ill.: Dryden Press, 1973), p. 70.
5. "A president who was truly above politics could not do his job. If a president wants to persuade Congress to adopt his policies and programs, he will have to execute the role of political leader." Robert A. Dahl, *Democracy in the United States,* 4th ed. (Chicago: Rand McNally, 1981), p. 84. "The acid test of presidential leadership of Congress lies in his political achievements, to which his constitutional powers of leadership are ancillary." Rowland Egger, *The President of the United States,* 2d ed. (New York: McGraw-Hill, 1972), p. 171. "The role of political brokering is central to the entire political process. It is the essence of the job of Presidents, and performing it occupies most of their time." Roger Hilsman, *To Govern America* (New York: Harper & Row, 1979), p. 81. "The president's primary task is leadership, setting national goals and priorities and mobilizing public support for his program." Harold Seidman, *Politics, Position and Power: The Dynamics of Federal Organization,* 3d ed. (New York: Oxford University Press, 1980), p. 325–26.

6. Theodore J. Lowi, *American Government: Incomplete Conquest* (Hinsdale, Ill.: Dryden Press, 1976), pp. 161–62.

7. George E. Reedy, *The Twilight of the Presidency* (New York: New American Library, 1970), p. 148.

8. Hilsman, *To Govern America*, p. 11.

9. James W. Davis, Jr., *The National Executive Branch* (New York: Free Press, 1970), p. 122.

10. Grant McConnell, *The Modern Presidency*, 2d ed. (New York: St. Martin's Press, 1976), pp. 99–100.

11. Stephen Hess, *Organizing the Presidency* (Washington, D.C.: Brookings Institution, 1976), p. 147.

12. Philippa Strum, *Presidential Power and American Democracy*, 2d ed. (Santa Monica, Calif.: Goodyear, 1979), p. 142.

13. Erwin C. Hargrove, *Presidential Leadership: Personality and Political Style* (New York: Macmillan, 1966), p. 153.

14. Aaron Wildavsky, "System is to Politics as Morality is to Man: A Sermon on the Presidency," in Aaron Wildavsky, *Perspectives on the Presidency* (Boston: Little, Brown, 1975), pp. 526, 538.

15. Thomas E. Cronin, *The State of the Presidency*, 2d ed. (Boston: Little, Brown, 1980), p. 168.

16. William L. Morrow, *Public Administration: Politics, Policy, and the Political System*, 2d ed. (New York: Random House, 1980), p. 3.

17. "The president is a figure symbolic of national purpose: he is also a human being. . . . Perhaps the chief constant is that the president must prove successful as a politician before he can attain this highest elective office. . . . To talk of the President as the 'people's choice' is to use extremely loose language. . . . Actually he is the product of a combination of political circumstances. . . . Moreover, there is no guarantee that the political coalition which made his election possible will hold together long enough to carry through to consummation any program that may have been projected. . . . The candidate appeals to the voters at large for his election, yet once in office he is dependent upon Congress for the realization of his program." Pendleton Herring, *Presidential Leadership* (New York: Farrar and Rinehart, 1940), pp. 1–2. "The President of the United States is the most continuously watched and the most intensely accountable public official in the world." McGeorge Bundy, *The Strength of Government* (Cambridge, Mass.: Harvard University Press, 1968), p. 57.

18. Harold D. Lasswell, *Power and Personality* (New York: Norton, 1948).

19. "Skill has two components: a sensitivity to power relationships and the ability to act to maximize personal, that is, Presidential, power in each of these areas," that is, public opinion, Congress, and the bureaucracy. Erwin C. Hargrove, *Presidential Leadership: Personality and Political Style* (New York: Macmillan, 1966), p. 2.

20. Richard E. Neustadt, *Presidential Power: The Politics of Leadership* (New York: John Wiley, 1960), pp. 10, 32–37.

21. Hargrove, *Presidential Leadership*, pp. 8–9, 144.

22. Ibid., p. 2.

23. Dorothy B. James, *The Contemporary Presidency*, 2d ed. (Indianapolis:

Bobbs-Merrill, 1974), p. 313.

24. Strum, *Presidential Power*, p. 151.

25. James MacGregor Burns, *Leadership* (New York: Harper & Row, 1978), pp. 252, 255–397.

26. Douglas Yates, "The Roots of American Leadership: Political Style and Policy Consequences," in Walter Dean Burnham and Martha Wagner Weinberg, eds., *American Politics and Public Policy* (Cambridge, Mass.: MIT Press, 1978), p. 144.

27. Hargrove, *Presidential Leadership*, p. 1.

28. Ibid.

29. James D. Barber, *Presidential Character: Predicting Performance in the White House* (Englewood Cliffs, N.J.: Prentice-Hall, 1972), pp. 3–11.

30. Ibid., pp. 11–14.

31. Ibid., pp. 14, 58, 145, 173, 209, 247, 293.

32. Nelson W. Polsby, *Congress and the Presidency*, 3d ed. (Englewood Cliffs, N.J.: Prentice-Hall, 1976), p. 18.

33. Emmet John Hughes, *The Living Presidency* (New York: Coward, McCann and Geoghegan, 1972), pp. 179–80.

34. Neustadt, *Presidential Power*, p. 6.

35. Mullen, *Presidential Power and Politics*, p. 251.

36. Barber, *Presidential Character*, p. 446.

37. Herring, *Presidential Leadership*, p. 111–12.

38. David B. Truman, *The Governmental Process* (New York: Knopf, 1951), p. 408.

39. "Today the President and his advisers in the executive department are alone qualified to undertake the immense task of formulating a comprehensive and coherent legislative program for the nation. The task of the President is no longer confined to executing the laws enacted by Congress; he must also provide leadership in legislation." George B. Galloway, *The Legislative Process in Congress* (New York: Crowell, 1953), p. 426.

40. Cronin, *State of the Presidency*, p. 220.

41. Binkley, *President and Congress*, pp. 245–50.

42. Doris A. Graber, *Mass Media and American Politics* (Washington, D.C.: Congressional Quarterly Press, 1980), p. 195.

43. Cronin, *State of the Presidency*, p. 104.

10

Shared Responsibility
for Legislation

The American political system operates primarily on the basis of concurrent powers. One branch can do very little without the support and countenance of the others.

Louis Fisher[1]

In developing policies and setting out directions, the president must take into account the *systemic* nature of politics—the way institutions and political people connect and interact.

Arnold J. Meltsner[2]

Responsible government means a fusion of powers between the executive and legislative rather than a separation.

Harold M. Barger[3]

The group responsibility of the House of Representatives, the Senate, and the presidency includes composite public policy for foreign relations and security affairs as well as for domestic issues. This position may differ from the general assumption of many analysts who assert in varying degrees that the president determines policy in foreign/security matters. As noted earlier, the Constitution explicitly grants Congress several types of power with respect to external affairs.[4] The positions of the Supreme Court in this area will now be considered. The Court may not make its position entirely clear, but it seems to prefer that Congress and the president work together, and it strives hard to find that they do have the same policy.

This chapter and the next will review Court opinions that appear to take that approach. First, cases in which Congress clearly sets policy for the president will be examined, and the next chapter will deal with more complex situations. Foreign and military affairs will be emphasized because that is where congressional-presidential relations seem most crucial.

RELEVANT DIFFERENCES BETWEEN
PARLIAMENT AND CONGRESS

There seems to be a tendency among many political scientists to draw upon the constitutional theories of John Locke and Baron de Montesquieu with respect to foreign affairs policy. Their famous works on constitutional theory maintained that the monarchical executive could legislate in the area of foreign affairs.[5]

Locke and Montesquieu dealt with the laws of England between approximately 1680 and 1740,[6] and there are several factors that make their ideas inappropriate to the allocation of authority between the Congress and the president. One of these is the contrast between the English system at the time of its revolution (1688) and the U.S. situation at the time of the 1787 convention.[7]

Locke accepted the idea of hereditary royalty and nobility, and Montesquieu insisted upon both. Also, the English system was built upon the idea of monarchical rule. England had had kings for almost a thousand years. Their relative power went up and down. The English Civil War of the 1640s and the Revolution of 1688 resulted in scaling down the authority and power of the king.[8]

Locke and Montesquieu allowed the monarch to be, in effect, the legislator of the law of nations, as a part of a general plan to deny him law-making power in domestic political matters.[9] Also, this was the start of a curtailment trend. There were additional reductions several times during the period between 1688 and 1787. George III may have tried to recover some of the king's authority, but his very attempt hastened the decline of the monarchy.

England and the United States differed much in their developmental roots and growth. English rule was monarchical whether it was Saxon, Dane, or Norman. Moreover, the kings had councils and they respected them. The Magna Carta was an accommodation between the king and the great barons. The two houses of Parliament evolved out of the small and large councils. In fact, the House of Commons emerged when moral support of the middle class was needed for new types of taxation. The Tudors (1485–1603) were the strongest dynasty, probably because Henry VII, Henry VIII, and Elizabeth were skilled at political reconciliation. The succeeding dynasty, the Stuarts, began the decline of the monarchy. But the kings were the ones who founded and raised England to its heights.

The development of national sovereignty in the United States was a different matter. U.S. independence and founding, it must again be emphasized, were guided by a series of loosely formed aristocratic Congresses—the Stamp Act Congress, the two Continental Congresses, the Confederation Congress, the congress-like Constitutional Convention, and the first bicameral Congress under the Constitution.[10]

The monocratic element of the United States' mixed system emerged not by invasion or by war of succession. It began when the Continental Congress in 1774 appointed George Washington to be commander in chief of the American forces. There was a national president before 1787, but he was the presiding officer of the Congress of state delegations. President and Congress were then a single institution.

THE CONSTITUTIONAL DOCTRINE OF NECESSARY ACTION

One of the several ways in which the midconvention draft constitution of the Committee of Detail laid the groundwork for the elevation and expansion of the constitutional system was the set of provisions for presidential and congressional cooperation in the development of "necessary and proper" legislation.

In contrast to the cryptic, one-sentence authorizations of the Virginia Plan, the draft constitution introduced positive opportunities for the president and Congress to deal with new and challenging situations. It obliged the president to "recommend" to the consideration of Congress "such measures as he shall judge necessary and expedient."[11] Correspondingly, it authorized Congress "to make all laws that shall be necessary and proper for carrying into execution" enumerated powers of Congress, as well as other powers of the government of the United States, or its departments or officers.

This elevated not only the president and Congress but also the Constitution itself. It established and maintained the idea of the president and Congress working together to extend the dimensions of social order. It opened the door for the enlargement of common responsibilities as well as a stronger economic order.[12]

The first demonstration of its potentials was the debate within Washington's cabinet on the power of the central authority to establish the Bank of the United States with superior rights within the several states. The issue did not reach the Supreme Court until 1819 when the recharter of the bank was challenged by the State of Maryland.[13] At that point Chief Justice John Marshall became in effect one of the team of high-level policy expansionists. His opinion in that case includes his classic definition of "necessary and proper."

> Let the end be legitimate, let it be within the scope of the Constitution, and all means which are appropriate, which are plainly adapted to that end, which are not prohibited, but consistent with the letter and spirit of the Constitution, are constitutional.[14]

The leading constitutional expert at midcentury, Edward S. Corwin, calls the necessary and proper provision, the "coefficient clause," and asserts that "this provision gives Congress a share in the responsibilities lodged in other departments." He also states, "Conversely, where necessary for the efficient execution of its own powers, Congress may delegate some measure of legislative power to other departments."[15]

Corwin observes that the provision authorized Congress to organize the federal judicial system, to control the national economy, and to establish monetary and fiscal controls, and to enact "a large body of law defining and punishing crimes."[16] With a government of this scope and complexity, the problems of legislation, execution, and representation tend to merge and become interdependent, which gives group responsibility to the elected institutions in the role of public policy superstructure.

SUPREME COURT OPINIONS ON LEGISLATIVE POWER

The common responsibility of the houses of Congress and the presidency with respect to legislation has been affected at times by the actions of the Supreme Court. These cases may bear upon the meaning of the doctrine of separated powers, but few have dealt with the principle directly. The opinions have been varied in their nature and impact. The total net effect seems to have been more favorable to Congress than the presidency, but often a decision supporting congressional authority has the effect of sustaining presidential activity.

The early opinions appear to be of limited value. An 1800 decision stated that "whenever the legislative power of a government is undefined, it includes the judicial and executive attributes."[17] It is hard to imagine the Supreme Court making such a statement in this century or even in most of the nineteenth.

The 1803 decision in which the Court held an act of Congress contrary to the Constitution concerned legislation that sought to enlarge the authority of the Supreme Court to issue the writ of mandamus.[18] The decision restricts the Court's own authority and saved it from the embarrassment of trying to take action against the regime of President Jefferson.[19]

An 1816 opinion used the three-power separation doctrine to enlarge the jurisdiction of the Court. The action involved the authority of the Supreme Court to deal with cases arising in the courts of Virginia. The Court said that the national judiciary has a right to hear cases that arose in the state courts. Justice Story explained:

> The object of the constitution was to establish three great departments of government; the legislative, the executive and the judicial departments. The first was to pass laws, the second to approve and execute them, and the third to expound and enforce them. Without the latter it would be impossible to carry into effect some of the express provisions of the constitution.[20]

The last was Story's basis for asserting that the Supreme Court necessarily has the full measure of judicial power defined in the Constitution. John Marshall made a similar assertion in an 1824 opinion.[21] Later the Court held that Congress could set up courts with less than the total constitutionally defined judicial power.

John Marshall in an 1825 opinion approved a pattern of congressional delegation of discretionary authority that had an effect, both long and large, upon the relations of Congress and both the president and the executive branch. However, the immediate case concerned congressional delegation to the judiciary.

Also, in his opinion in *Wayman v. Southard* (1825), Marshall set forth a simple statement of the threefold formula of parallel allocation. The particular issue was whether state laws on the execution of judgments applied in the federal courts, and that turned in part on the authority of Congress to grant the federal courts the right to promulgate rules of procedure that Congress itself could have enacted.[22]

Chief Justice Marshall asserted that "the legislature makes, the executive executes, and the judiciary construes the law," and he concluded that the congressional grant of rule-making authority to the federal courts was not invalid because Congress had not delegated what is "strictly and exclusively legislative." The decision aided the national judiciary against the states and preserved the theory of separate functions by reserving an undefined concept of what is exclusively legislative. Later, the Court approved delegations of congressional discretion to other official institutions, and this in time allowed Congress to delegate much discretion to the president and the several executive departments and agencies.

The Supreme Court used the separate power formula again in 1867 to sustain self-limitation. This was in a situation in which the State of Mississippi had sought an injunction against the execution of the Reconstruction Acts of Congress on the ground that the statutes were unconstitutional. The Court held that it could not enjoin the president from executing acts of Congress. It said that injunctions are limited to ministerial duties, and here the duty was not of that type. A similar case was brought by the State of Georgia against the secretary of war, and the Court reached a similar result. The denial of an injunction is not limited to suits against the president.[23]

In one respect these decisions are similar to the refusals of the Court to consider "nonjuridical" issues. They result in the houses of Congress and the presidency having determination of the matter.[24]

CONGRESSIONAL DELEGATION IN FOREIGN AFFAIRS

The Supreme Court also has approved delegations by Congress of discretionary authority to the president in matters relating to foreign affairs, even though the president can decide, in fact, whether the law really takes effect. This is one of the principal processes by which the houses of Congress and the presidency may meet their common responsibilities.

The foremost decision of this type is that concerning the *Curtiss-Wright Export Corporation* (1936).[25] The opinion of Justice Sutherland in this case is often quoted because of what he said about presidential authority in foreign affairs, but we need to keep in mind that this was not a situation in which the White House was acting independently of Congress but rather involved an action by Congress extending authority to the president to decide whether a certain foreign policy action should be taken.[26]

The *Curtiss-Wright* case concerned a joint resolution of Congress prohibiting the sale of arms to Bolivia and Paraguay, which were engaged in a border war, *if* the president of the United States should issue a proclamation that such a ban would aid the reestablishment of peace in the area.

The president issued such a proclamation, and *Curtiss-Wright* was charged with violating that joint resolution. The corporation sought to avoid liability by claiming that the joint resolution was an undue delegation of authority to the president. The corporation asserted in part that the congressional action was contrary to the Tenth Amendment because it invaded the reserved power of the states.

The issue of nation-state division of legislative authority gave rise to an inquiry into the transfer of national sovereignty at the time of the American independence from Great Britain in the period of 1776–83. The opinion of Justice George Sutherland for the Court made this clear for the first time. It made a sharp distinction between internal and external sovereignty of the United States and also between the powers of the federal government with respect to foreign or external affairs and those with respect to domestic or internal affairs:

> Whether, if the Joint Resolution had related solely to internal affairs, it would be open to the challenge that it constituted an unlawful delegation of legislative power to the Executive, we find it unnecessary to determine. The whole aim of the resolution is to affect a situation entirely external to the United States, and falling within the category of foreign affairs.
>
> The determination which we are called to make, therefore, is whether the Joint Resolution, as applied to that situation, is vulnerable to attack under the rule that forbids a delegation of the lawmaking power. In other words, assuming (but not deciding) that the challenged delegation, if it were confined to internal affairs, would be invalid, may it nevertheless be sustained on the ground that its exclusive aim is to afford a remedy for a hurtful condition within foreign territory?[27]

The court said that it would first consider the differences between "the power of the federal government in respect of foreign or external affairs and those in respect of domestic or internal affairs."

> The two classes of powers are different, both in respect of their origin and their nature. The broad statement that the federal government can exercise no powers except those specifically enumerated in the Constitution, and such implied powers as are necessary and proper to carry into effect the enumerated powers, is categorically true only in respect of our internal affairs.
>
> In that field, the primary purpose of the Constitution was to carve from the general mass of legislative powers *then possessed by the states* such portions as it was thought desirable to vest in the federal government, leaving those not included in the enumeration still in the states. . . . since the states severally never possessed international powers, such powers could not have been carved from the mass of state powers but obviously were transmitted to the United States from some other source.[28]

Justice Sutherland pointed out that during the colonial period, the external powers were possessed entirely by the crown and were entirely under its control, and not that of the colonies.

> As a result of the separation from Great Britain by the colonies, acting as a unit, the powers of external sovereignty passed from the Crown not to the colonies severally, but to the colonies in their collective and corporate capacity as the United States of America. Even before the Declaration [of Independence], the colonies were a unit in foreign affairs, acting through a common agency—namely, the Continental Congress, composed of delegates from the thirteen colonies.
>
> That agency exercised the powers of war and peace, raised an army, created a navy, and finally adopted the Declaration of Independence. Rulers come and go; governments end and forms of government change; but sovereignty survives. A political society cannot endure without a supreme will somewhere. Sovereignty is never held in suspense. When, therefore, the external sovereignty of Great Britain in respect of the colonies ceased, it immediately passed to the Union.[29]

The opinion of Justice Sutherland is also novel in its identification of a nonconstitutional source of foreign affairs authority:

It results that the investment of the federal government with the powers of external sovereignty did not depend upon the affirmative grants of the Constitution. The powers to declare and wage war, to conclude peace, to make treaties, to maintain diplomatic relations with other sovereignties, if they had never been mentioned in the Constitution, would have vested in the federal government as necessary concomitants of nationality. . . .

As a member of the family of nations, the right and power of the United States in that field are equal to the right and power of the other members of the international family. Otherwise, the United States is not completely sovereign. . . .[30]

But in this case, Congress had set the foreign policy and the conditions of action for the President. Sutherland continued:

In this vast external realm, with its important, complicated, delicate and manifold problems, the President alone has the power to speak or listen as a representative of the nation. He *makes* treaties with the advice and consent of the Senate; but he alone negotiates. Into the field of negotiation the Senate cannot intrude and Congress itself is powerless to invade it. . . .[31]

Yet "negotiation" is not the whole activity of making foreign policy. It may be made within the White House and the Capitol as well as in channels of communication. Also, there may be a principal-agent relationship, in which Congress is the principal and the president the agent. But the issue at hand is whether Congress delegated too much authority to the president. The Court may be saying that the president has some authority that did not come from Congress and thus we should not claim improper delegation. Justice Sutherland continues:

It is important to bear in mind that we are here dealing not alone with an authority vested in the President by an exertion of legislative power, but with such an authority plus the very delicate, plenary and exclusive power of the President as the sole organ of the federal government in the field of international relations—a power which does not require as a basis for its exercise an act of Congress, but which, of course, like every other governmental power must be exercised in *subordination* to the applicable provisions of the Constitution.

It is quite apparent that if, in the maintenance of our international relations, embarrassment—perhaps serious embarrassment—is to be avoided and success for our aims achieved, congressional legislation which is to be made effective through negotiation and inquiry within the international field must often accord to the President a degree of discretion and freedom from statutory restriction which would not be admissible were domestic affairs alone involved [emphasis added].[32]

The Court pointed out that the president has "the better opportunity of knowing the conditions" in foreign countries, especially in time of war because the president has "agents" in the form of diplomatic and consular officers. Yet the advantage is relative: the Court stating that this opportunity to know facts is *better*. Presidential sources of information were particularly important in that case because the joint resolution of Congress expressly left it up to the president to decide whether export of war materiel to the area in South America would endanger peace.

Justice Sutherland referred to a presidential refusal to give the House of Representatives requested information. This concerned the Jay Treaty of 1794 in which President Washington's denial of information was based on the fact that the House had no constitutional role in the treaty procedure, as did the Senate. The House was being asked to appropriate funds necessary to give effect to the treaty.[33] But the information requested was the instruction to Jay in negotiating the treaty, and that probably had a political factor more than a financial one. The House finally appropriated the necessary funds. The president won politically or pragmatically, and Justice Sutherland seems to be using that as a legal precedent.

The Court opinion gives even more weight to the practice of Congress in granting discretion to the president in matters of foreign relations. One example is the following statement:

Practically every volume of the United States Statutes contains one or more acts or joint resolutions of Congress authorizing action by the President in respect of subjects affecting foreign relations, which either leave the exercise of the power to his unrestricted judgment, or provide a standard far more general than that which has always been considered requisite with regard to domestic affairs.[34]

Yet the Court in a 1965 decision treated the foreign affairs difference as only relative.[35] That case concerned passport travel restrictions on travel to communist countries. In upholding the limitations, the Supreme Court referred to the last quoted statement and said: "This does not mean that simply because a statute deals with foreign relations, it can grant the Executive totally unrestricted freedom of choice."[36] The Court remarked that, in matters of foreign affairs, Congress "must of necessity paint with a brush broader than that it customarily wields in domestic areas."[37] The difference is relative; its source is less in the inherent character of the subject than in the surrounding conditions.

NOTES

1. Louis Fisher, *The Politics of Shared Power: Congress and the Executive* (Washington, D.C.: Congressional Quarterly Press, 1981), p. 11.

2. Arnold J. Meltsner, ed., *Politics and the Oval Office: Toward Presidential Governance* (San Francisco: Institute of Contemporary Studies, 1981), p. 287.

3. Harold M. Barger, *The Impossible Presidency* (Glenview, Ill.: Scott, Foresman, 1984), p. 97.

4. See the section entitled "Broad Powers over External Sovereignty" in Chapter 5.

5. Peter Laslett, ed., *Locke's Two Treatises of Government* (Cambridge: University Press, 1960); Baron de Montesquieu, *The Spirit of the Laws* (New York: Hafner, 1949).

6. See, in general, Colin R. Lovell, *English Constitutional and Legal History* (New York: Oxford University Press, 1962), pp. 174–228, 229–81, 282–335.

7. See Chapter 2.

8. Lovell, *Constitutional and Legal History*, pp. 282–335.

9. See Laslett, *Locke's Two Treatises*; Montesquieu, *Spirit of the Laws.*

10. See the section entitled "Congresses of the American Founding Period" in Chapter 2.

11. See the section entitled "Double Emergence of the Presidency" in Chapter 4.

12. See the section entitled "Expanded Pattern of the Draft Constitution" in Chapter 4.

13. Alfred H. Kelly and Winfred A. Harbison, *The American Constitution: Its Origins and Development*, 4th ed. (New York: Norton, 1970), pp. 288–92.

14. Ibid., p. 290.

15. Edward S. Corwin, ed., *The Constitution of the United States of America: Analysis and Interpretation* (Washington, D.C.: Government Printing Office,

1953), pp. 307–9.

16. Ibid., p. 308.
17. *Cooper v. Telfair,* 4 Dallas 14, 15–16 (1800).
18. *Marbury v. Madison,* 1 Cranch 137 (1803).
19. Kelly and Harbison, *American Constitution,* pp. 226–30.
20. *Martin v. Hunter's Lessee,* 1 Wheaton 304, 329 (1816).
21. *Osborn v. The Bank of the United States,* 9 Wheaton 738, 819 (1824).
22. *Wayman v. Southard,* 10 Wheaton 1, 42, 46 (1825).
23. *Mississippi v. Johnson,* 4 Wallace 475, 479 (1867); *Georgia v. Stanton,* 6 Wall 50 (1868).
24. See the section entitled "Final Determination of Nonjuridical Issues" in Chapter 12.
25. *United States v. Curtiss-Wright Export Corp.,* 299 U.S. 304 (1936).
26. See Chapter 6.
27. *United States v. Curtiss-Wright Export Corp.,* 299 U.S. 304, 315.
28. Ibid., pp. 315–16.
29. Ibid., p. 316.
30. Ibid., p. 318.
31. Ibid., p. 319.
32. Ibid.
33. Ibid., p. 320.
34. Ibid., p. 324.
35. *Zemel v. Rusk,* 381 U.S. 1 (1965).
36. Ibid., p. 17.
37. Ibid.

11

Shared Responsibility
for Legitimation

Congress . . . enhances the legitimacy of governmental decisions by
ensuring that decisions are reached through publicly accepted procedures and implemented by responsible agents. It helps to form the
opinion of a democratic electorate and enhance popular participation in the complicated processes of government. In defining public
policy, it adapts the structure of governmental institutions to a
steadily changing political environment.

John S. Saloma III[1]

Even where his authority is presumably great, in foreign affairs and
as Commander in Chief, the President depends on Congressional
support.

Louis W. Koenig[2]

Lawmaking is slow because the process of reconciliation is slow,
inevitably so in an institution with limited hierarchy, decentralized
power, and weak parties. . . . The slow pace of Congress is consistent
with its purpose; it is, after all, primarily a deliberative assembly, not
commonly expected to make quick decisions.

William J. Keefe[3]

The stickiest problem of U.S. constitutional democracy is, as
noted several times, how a slow-acting Congress can guide a fast-
acting president. Many scholarly and journalistic analysts seem to dis-
miss the idea of congressional participation and leave foreign/security
policy to the presidency.

This book makes three suggestions. One is that the faults of Congress derive from its sacred role of protecting the people. Democracy entails district identification and representation, which makes inefficiency inevitable. Two types of action may be feasible. One is emergency action in advance, and the other is legitimation in retrospect. There is much more of each than is commonly recognized. During World War II emergency legislation was so extensive that it was at least a dozen years before the emergencies were terminated officially.

This chapter will review court opinions with respect to the pros and cons of ratification. Most of the discussion will concern opinions of the Supreme Court and the courts of appeals.

THE CONSTITUTIONALITY OF LEGITIMATION

Legitimation is as constitutional as the Constitution. It is also as old as the Constitution of 1787. The Constitution took effect, not according to the prior formula set when it was proposed, but rather pursuant to one devised by the convention in its closing days. This is recognized by the leading constitutional scholar of this century, Edward S. Corwin:

> The Articles of Confederation provided for their own amendment only by unanimous consent of the thirteen States, given through their legislatures. The provision made for the going into effect of the Constitution upon its ratification by *nine* States, given through *conventions* called for that purpose, clearly indicates the establishment of the Constitution to have been, in the legal sense, an act of revolution.[4]

The present-day successor to Professor Corwin, J. W. Peltason, says of the ratification process that "the delegates to the Convention boldly assumed power to exceed their mandate."[5]

James Madison in the *Federalist Letter No. 37* touches upon this legitimation process. He says that the purpose of the *Federalist* is to determine the merits of the Constitution and "the expediency of adopting it."[6] That thought does not degrade the Constitution, but rather enables "expedience." The standard may be "necessity" more than "expediency." Madison defended each part and the whole of the Constitution on the grounds of "necessity."[7] We have seen that the concept dominated the 1787 proceedings from start to finish.

The call of the convention by the Confederation Congress on February 21, 1787, recited "the inefficiency of the federal government and the necessity of devising such farther provisions as shall render the same adequate to the exigencies of the Union." The resolution recommended that representatives of the states meet and report to the Congress such "alterations and amendments" as they "shall judge proper and necessary to render [the Articles of Confederation] adequate to the preservation and support of the Union."[8]

When the convention met on May 29, 1787, Governor Randolph presented a set of 15 resolutions to correct and enlarge the Articles of Confederation. But two of the resolutions (6 and 12) referred to "the articles of Union." The next day Randolph explained that a "federal" union would not accomplish the objects proposed and that "a *national* Government ought to be established consisting of a *supreme* Legislative, Executive and Judiciary."[9] Some delegates were disturbed by the terms *national* and *supreme*. Within two or three weeks, antinational forces began to mobilize, and there was reduced use of the term *national*.[10] In fact, in the ratification efforts the word *federal* was brought back with a new meaning.[11]

The possibility of conflict between the terms *Articles of Confederation* and *Articles of Union* was averted on July 24 when the convention referred the resolutions thus far adopted to the Committee of Detail to draft a "constitution."[12] Thus, the Constitution may indicate a neutral document.

It has been pointed out a number of times that the provision that is most likely to assure the Constitution a long life is the authorization of Congress to enact "necessary and proper" laws.[13]

SUPREME COURT REJECTION OF PRESIDENTIAL INDEPENDENCE

The second landmark decision of the Supreme Court on the policy-making interactions of the elected institutions "called forth the full measure of the Court's condemnation of emergency government."[14] The case involved the attempt of President Truman to seize strike-threatened steel mills during the Korean War.

On almost all sides the events were unsatisfactory. Basically, the conflict was between a "left" president and a "right" Congress on how to regulate labor unions. Congress had enacted the Taft-Hartley Act with provisions for dealing with emergencies. The president did not use that procedure but acted independently of the legislation.[15] The Supreme Court decided six to three against the president. The result may illustrate high-level checks and balances in juridical cases—when Congress and the president differ, the Supreme Court seems most apt to favor bicameral congressional action.

The explanation of the decision by the Supreme Court was not at all neat. Justice Black wrote the opinion for the Court, but each of the other five justices who made up the majority wrote a concurring opinion. Later, much attention will be given to that of Justice Jackson. It includes a threefold classification of congressional-presidential relationships that stresses the considerable dependence of the president upon actions of Congress.

Justice Black's opinion for the Court pointed out that when the Taft-Hartley legislation was under consideration during 1947 Congress rejected an authorization of governmental seizure of plants in cases of emergency. Instead, the enactment sought to bring about settlements by mediation, conciliation, investigation, and public reports. "In some instances temporary injunctions were authorized to provide cooling-off periods."[16]

In the case at hand, concerning the *Youngstown Sheet and Tube Company,* the labor dispute had begun in 1951, the cooling-off period had passed, and a Wage Stabilization Board effort at compromise had failed. The United Steel Workers union called a nationwide strike to begin on April 9, 1952. On the eve of the walkout, President Truman issued an executive order to the secretary of commerce, Charles Sawyer, to take possession of the steel mills and operate them. When the secretary issued a seizure order the steel companies attacked the constitutionality of the seizure in the courts. A district court judge enjoined the secretary, and a court of appeals stayed the injunction. The Supreme Court granted certiorari and 30 days later handed down its decision.

The relevant portions of Justice Black's opinion for the Court were that, if the president had power to issue the seizure order, it must come from an act of Congress or from the Constitution itself,[17] that there was no statute giving express or implied power, and that the government-cited cases upholding broad powers in military commanders engaged in day-to-day fighting in a theater of war were not applicable:

Even though "theater of war" be an expanding concept, we cannot with faithfulness to our constitutional system hold that the Commander in Chief of the Armed Forces has the ultimate power as such to take possession of private property in order to keep labor disputes from stopping production. This is a job for the Nation's lawmakers, not for its military authorities.

Nor can the seizure order be sustained because of the several constitutional provisions that grant executive power to the President. In the framework of our Constitution, the President's power to see that the laws are faithfully executed refutes the idea that he is to be a lawmaker. The Constitution limits his functions in the law-making process to the recommending of laws he thinks wise and the vetoing of laws he thinks bad. And the Constitution is neither silent nor equivocal about who shall make laws which the President is to execute.[18]

This is, of course, a restricted concept of "executive power." It does not look back to the idea of kings, or philosophers, or philosopher-kings. Justice Frankfurter expressed similar ideas in his concurring opinion. Justice Douglas summarized his views and those of Justices Black and Frankfurter with the comment that "the power to execute the laws starts and ends with the laws Congress has enacted."[19]

This book concerns primarily the high policy responsibility of the three elected institutions; the portion of the opinions in the *Youngstown* case that is most relevant here is that part of a concurring opinion that classified the authority relationships of Congress and the president.

CLASSIFICATION OF
CONGRESSIONAL-PRESIDENTIAL RELATIONSHIPS

The concurring opinion of Supreme Court Justice Robert Jackson in the *Youngstown* steel seizure case included this assessment and classification of presidential authority:

The actual art of governing under our Constitution does not and cannot conform to judicial definitions of the power of any of its branches based on isolated clauses or even single Articles torn from context. While the Constitution diffuses power the better to secure liberty, it also contemplates that practice will integrate the dispersed powers into a workable government. It enjoins upon its branches separateness but interdependence, autonomy but reciprocity.

Presidential powers are not fixed but fluctuate, depending upon their disjunction or conjunction with those of Congress. We may well begin by a somewhat over-simplified grouping of practical situations in which a President may doubt, or others may challenge, his powers, and by distinguishing roughly the legal consequences of this factor of relativity.

1. When the President acts pursuant to an express or implied authorization of Congress, his authority is at its maximum, for it includes all that he possesses in his own right plus all that Congress can delegate. In these circumstances, and in these only, may he be said (for what it may be worth) to personify the federal sovereignty. If his act is held unconstitutional under these circumstances, it usually means that the Federal Government as an undivided whole lacks power.

A seizure executed by the President pursuant to an Act of Congress would be supported by the strongest of presumptions and the widest latitude of judicial interpretation, and the burden of persuasion would rest heavily upon any who might attack it.

2. When the President acts in absence of either a congressional grant or denial of authority, he can only rely upon his own independent powers, but there is a zone of twilight in which he and Congress may have concurrent authority, or in which its distribution is uncertain. Therefore, Congressional inertia, indifference or quiescence may sometimes, at least as a practical matter, enable, if not invite, measures on independent presidential responsibility. In this area, any actual test of power is likely to depend on the imperatives of events and contemporary imponderables rather than on abstract theories of law.

3. When the President takes measures incompatible with the expressed or implied will of Congress, his power is at its lowest ebb, for then he can rely only upon his own constitutional powers minus any constitutional powers of Congress over the matter. Courts can sustain exclusive Presidential control in such a case only by disabling the Congress from acting upon the subject. Presidential claim to a power at once so conclusive and preclusive must be scrutinized with caution, for what is at stake is the equilibrium established by our constitutional system.

Into which of these classifications does this executive seizure of the steel industry fit? It is eliminated from the first by admission, for it is conceded that no congressional authorization exists for this seizure. That takes away also the support of the many precedents and declarations which were made in relation, and must be confined, to this category.

Can it be defended under flexible texts available to the second category? It seems clearly eliminated from that class because Congress has not left seizure of private property an open field but has covered it by three statutory policies inconsistent with this seizure....

This leaves the current seizure to be justified under the third grouping, where it can be supported only by any remainder of executive power after subtraction of such powers as Congress may have over the subject. In short, we can sustain the President only by holding that seizure of such strike-bound industries is within his domain and beyond control by Congress. Thus, this Court's first review of such seizures occurs under circumstances which leave Presidential power most vulnerable to attack and in the least favorable of possible constitutional postures.[20]

The threefold classification of presidential-congressional relationships was presented in the concurring opinion of Justice Jackson in the *Youngstown* case,[21] but the first category was approved by the Court in a 1981 decision concerning the action of President Carter at the time of the Iranian capture of U.S. diplomatic personnel.[22]

In 1981, the Court said that Congress had accepted the White House practice of using executive agreements in such situations. A Carter presidential order had nullified attachments by U.S. citizens on Iranian assets and directed persons holding such assets to transfer them to the Federal Reserve Bank of New York for ultimate transfer to Iran in the arrangement for the release of the hostages. The frozen assets served as a "bargaining chip" by the president when dealing with the Iranian government. The opinion of the Court included this statement:

Because the President's action in nullifying the attachments and ordering the transfer of the assets was taken pursuant to specific congressional authorization, it is "supported by the strongest of presumptions and the widest latitude of judicial interpretation, and the burden of persuasion would rest heavily upon any who might attack it."[23]

The quoted language in the last part of the statement of the Court was taken by Justice Rehnquist from the *Youngstown* opinion of Justice Jackson. It was part of his description of the first category in which there is express or implied authorization by Congress of the presidential action. This use in the opinion for the Court indicates general approval of Jackson's classification in the earlier case.

In that situation, President Carter acted pursuant to the International Emergency Economic Powers Act (IEEPA) (50 USCS Sec. 1701). It declared a national emergency on November 14, 1979, and blocked the removal or transfer of certain property of the Iranian government. The Court determined that that statute authorized the president to nullify attachments and order transfer of the Iranian assets. The Court held that the act did not authorize the president to suspend claims in U.S. courts. This indicates how dependent presidential authority may be upon the interpretation of a statute and shows that even here the president may not have a broad range of authority.

The Court indicated that it was moved in certain conclusions by "a history of congressional acquiescence in conduct of the sort engaged in by the President." The Court found that "the United States has repeatedly exercised its sovereign authority, to settle the claims of its nationals against foreign countries." It found also that while such settlements are sometimes made by treaty, "there has also been a long-standing practice of settling such claims by executive agreement without the advice and consent of the Senate." The Court found after the fact approval or legitimation: "Crucial to our decision today is the conclusion that Congress has implicitly approved the practice of claim settlement by executive agreement."[24] The Court pointed out that the Congress has amended the International Claims Settlement Act to facilitate the settlement of claims against Vietnam. The Court concluded that the legislative history of the IEEPA further reveals that Congress has accepted the authority of the executive to enter into settlement agreements. Thus, the Supreme Court finds congressional approval in the indirect and implied force of a number of events as well as in express specific language. The Court recognized that the IEEPA was enacted "to provide some limitation on the President's emergency powers" but indicated that the act did not interfere with the authority of the president to settle claims.[25]

This evaluation may be similar to assessment of the War Powers Act of 1973. It imposes some limitation upon the use of the armed forces, but it also provides support for the limited use of the military.

The decision in the Iranian claims case may furnish support for the threefold classification of Justice Jackson in the *Youngstown* case. Congressional support for presidential actions may be express, or indirect, or it may be lacking. Congressional action is often complex or confusing, but the Court seems anxious to find some congressional approval or acceptance of presidential action. If Congress does support the president to some appreciable degree, then it is easier for the Court to approve the presidential action, or at least the Court is more willing to do so.

The Civil War of the 1860s provided several instances of doubtful actions by President Lincoln. Cases of military trials outside the active theater of war reached the Supreme Court. In one it said that it could not review decisions of a military tribunal.[26] In another the Court held that a military trial was improper in an area where the civilian courts were still open.[27] In this last instance, Congress may have been at fault in authorizing military commissions in such areas.

While the Supreme Court seems eager to find congressional support for presidential actions, scholarly analysts appear more likely to judge presidents on their initiative and their demands. World Wars I and II involved such a governmental and industrial effort that there was disorder all around. Legislation, execution, administration, and industrial operation were all vast and complex, and extraordinary actions were commonplace.

Scholarly accounts tend to focus upon the president and to consider expanded activity a mark of "prerogative" or even "dictatorship." Analysts find the high point to be Franklin Roosevelt's threat on September 7, 1942, to set aside a ceiling-price section of the Emergency Price Control Act, if Congress did not repeal the provision. But Congress repealed it, and the president did not need to act. This is said to be "a presidential claim of a right of executive nullification" because a statute did not conform to the president's policy and is called a "claim to executive prerogative" unsurpassed in all U.S. history.[28] But it was only a claim. If the presidential threat was extraordinary, the congressional capitulation was also remarkable. The president did not ignore Congress, as Hamilton did in 1793; FDR threatened Congress—and succeeded. It may be necessary to look more at the congressional side of the encounter.

CONGRESSIONAL RATIFICATION OF LINCOLN'S PREACTION

The foremost instance of congressional approval of presidential initiative may be the action of Congress in 1861. This is also an outstanding example of legitimation, probably next in magnitude to the adoption of the 1787 Constitution. It came at the start of the War between the States. Lincoln had been elected president by less than 40 percent of the popular vote. The Republicans were a minority in Congress until enough southern states withdrew from the Union. By March 4, 1861, when the new president was inaugurated, seven states had seceded. Lincoln asserted he would strengthen the garrison at Fort Sumter, and on April 12, 1861 the Confederate forces bombarded it. What happened then is described in Wilfred Binkley's historical analysis, *President and Congress:*

> Thus the period of executive groping suddenly ended and was followed promptly by executive action so extraordinary as to challenge thus early in Lincoln's administration the Whig-Republican theory of the dominant place of Congress in the government. Congress, of course, was not in session. The available military forces were utterly inadequate for the vast emergency. But no sooner had Lincoln exhausted his constitutional and statutory authority than he proceeded to exceed it. For example, by a proclamation of May 3, 1861, he ordered the regular army increased by 22,714 officers and men and the navy by 18,000 and called for 42,034 volunteers for three years.[29]

The validity of Lincoln's action was questioned by "the temperate and loyal Republican, Senator John Sherman." Later, it was defended by a leading political scientist of the period, John W. Burgess, who based it upon the "spirit of the Constitution." Binkley calls that "a magic principle" under which the Constitution could be given "a more remarkable elasticity than John Marshall ever discovered." Binkley questions why Congress could not have been convened on May 3, 1861, the date of Lincoln's proclamation. Public opinion was confused until the April 12 attack on Fort Sumter, but that event "produced an instant and militant solidarity among Northerners that would have enabled the President to convene a prompt and willing Congress. Instead he set the date for the special session eleven weeks after the opening of hostilities."[30]

When the special session convened on July 4, 1861, President Lincoln invited Congress to grant him retroactive authority for what he had done. Lincoln called the measures "a popular demand and a public necessity, trusting then as now, that Congress would readily ratify them." Lincoln asserted that "nothing has been done *beyond the constitutional competence of Congress.*" On August 6, 1861,

Congress did ratify the president's actions. Binkley suggests that Congress acted "to save its own claim of authority." There apparently was some hesitation and dissatisfaction. Binkley indicates that some subsequent actions were also questionable.[31]

Whether the need for congressional ratification or approval had any restraint on Lincoln may be debatable. Lincoln did make a point that he did not exceed the constitutional power of Congress. Lincoln may have had congressional ratification in mind during the period that Congress was not in session and he was acting much like a legislator, and he may have kept within the limits of congressional authority in the hopes that that would increase the chances of ratification.

The Supreme Court, in the *Prize Cases,* stated that there was legislative approval for the war:

> If it were necessary to the technical existence of a war, that it should have a legislative sanction, we find it in almost every Act passed at the extraordinary session of the Legislature of 1861, which was wholly employed in enacting laws to enable the government to prosecute the war with vigor and efficiency.
>
> And finally, in 1861 we find Congress "*ex majore cautela*" and in anticipation of such astute objections, passing an Act "approving, legalizing and making valid all the acts, proclamations, and orders of the President, &c., as if they had been issued and done under the previous express authority and direction of the Congress of the United States."
>
> Without admitting that such an Act was necessary under the circumstances, it is plain that if the President had in any manner assumed powers which it was necessary should have the authority or sanction of Congress, that on the well known principle of law, "*omnis ratihabitio retrotrahitur et mandato equiparatur,*" this ratification has operated to perfectly cure the defect.[32]

The Supreme Court also said this "act of ratification" was not unconstitutional as *"ex post facto."* That "might possibly have some weight on the trial of an indictment in a criminal court" but is not "authoritative in a tribunal administering public and international law."[33] This is similar to our distinction here between the legal infrastructure and the policy superstructure.

CONGRESSIONAL PARTICIPATION IN THE VIETNAM WAR

There seems to be an instance of legitimation, that is, subsequent congressional approval, in the litigation involving the constitutional sufficiency of authority of the executive branch to wage war in Vietnam. The Supreme Court did not consider this question in itself, but it did deny a writ of certiorari with respect to decisions of the circuit courts of appeal.

The foremost opinion of a court of appeals may be *Orlando v. Laird,* and the companion case, *Berk v. Laird,* by the Court of Appeals fo the Second Circuit (New York). The plaintiffs contended that the Defense Department and army officials "exceeded their constitutional authority" by ordering the plaintiffs "to participate in a war not properly authorized by Congress."[34]

The plaintiffs contended that "the sufficiency of congressional authorization is a matter within juridical competence" of the courts, and that congressional appropriations and "other war-implementing enactments" are not sufficient authorization because "they lack an explicit authorization of particular hostilities." The government claimed that the issue is "a non-justiciable political question" and that "the military action was authorized and ratified by congressional appropriation."

The circuit court of appeals stated that "the constitutional delegation of the war-declaring power to the Congress contains a discoverable and manageable standard imposing on the Congress a duty of mutual participation in the prosecution of the war."[35] The circuit court's opinion presented these conclusions:

> Judicial scrutiny of that duty, therefore, is not foreclosed by the political questions doctrine. . . . the test is whether there is any action by the Congress sufficient to authorize or ratify the military activity in question. The evidentiary materials produced at the hearings in the district court clearly disclose that this test is satisfied.
>
> The Congress and the Executive have taken mutual and joint action in the prosecution and support of military operations in Southeast Asia from the beginning of these operations.[36]

The opinion notes the Tonkin Gulf Resolution of August 10, 1964, but did not limit its findings to that action.

Congress has ratified the executive's initiatives by appropriating billions of dollars to carry out military operations in Southeast Asia and by extending the Military Selective Service Act with full knowledge that persons conscripted under that Act had been, and would continue to be, sent to Vietnam. . . .

There is, therefore, no lack of clear evidence to support a conclusion that there was an abundance of continuing mutual participation in the prosecution of the war. Both branches collaborated in the endeavor, and neither could long maintain such a war without the concurrence and cooperation of the other. . . .[37]

The circuit court opinion also characterizes the "war power of Congress" as being more than the adoption of a declaration:

The framers intent to vest the war power in Congress is in no way defeated by permitting an inference of authorization from legislative action furnishing the manpower and materials of war for the protracted military operations in Southeast Asia. . . .

Beyond determining that there has been *some* mutual participation between the Congress and the President, which unquestionably exists here, with action by the Congress sufficient to authorize or ratify the military activity at issue, it is clear that the constitutional propriety of the means by which Congress has chosen to ratify and approve the protracted military operations in Southeast Asia is a political question. The form which congressional authorization should take is one of policy, committed to the discretion of the Congress and outside the power and competence of the judiciary. . . .[38]

This is a decision and opinion of the Court of Appeals for the Second Circuit. The Supreme Court denied certiorari. We cannot say that the higher court agrees fully, but it seems to be as close to an opinion of the Supreme Court as there is or is likely to be.

The circuit court found that Congress permitted and supported the Vietnam War. It said that there was "some mutual participation" of Congress and the president. In fact, it says that Congress did "ratify and approve" the military operations and the form of its action was beyond the competence of the judiciary.

In general, Congress and the presidency are different types of institutions with different modes of action. The diversity of Congress and the unity of the presidency can and do complement each other.

CONGRESSIONAL ABROGATION OF A TREATY

The constitutional authority of Congress to control foreign policy is illustrated also by its power to terminate at least the internal force of a treaty even though made by the president and approved by the Senate. The Supreme Court held that Congress had such authority in an 1890 decision upholding an act of Congress that contravened provisions of a treaty allowing the immigration of certain Chinese laborers.[39]

This situation shows how Congress can take action after the president has acted with approval of the Senate. Treaties in 1868 and 1880 dealt with those Chinese who had been in the United States and had returned to China. An act of Congress in 1888 nullified the effect of the treaties, at least as law within the United States.

The matter reached the Supreme Court and the opinion of Justice Grier for the Supreme Court explained its approval of the action of Congress:

> It must be conceded that the Act of 1888 is in contravention of express stipulations of the Treaty of 1868 and of the Supplemental Treaty of 1880, but it is not on that account invalid or to be restricted in its enforcement. The treaties were of no greater legal obligation than the Act of Congress. By the Constitution, laws made in pursuance thereof and treaties made under the authority of the United States are both declared to be the supreme law of the land, and no paramount authority is given to one over the other.
>
> A treaty, it is true, is in its nature a contract between nations, and is often merely promissory in its character, requiring legislation to carry its stipulations into effect. Such legislation will be open to future repeal or amendment. If the treaty operates by its own forces, and relates to a subject within the power of Congress, it can be deemed in that particular only the equivalent of a legislative Act, to be repealed or modified at the pleasure of Congress. In either case the last expression of the sovereign will must control.[40]

The Court pointed out that it had considered the effect of legislation upon conflicting treaty stipulations in the Head-Money cases, in 1884, and decided that a treaty is subject to such statutes as Congress may enact for its enforcement, modification, or repeal.[41]

Congressional actions of, in effect, repealing a treaty that had been made by the president and approved by the Senate indicate that subsequent action may be effective in influencing or changing the foreign policy of the United States in particular situations. Presidents may claim that subsequent action by Congress contrary to a treaty may embarrass the United States in its foreign relations. But the Supreme Court did not let that possibility change its decision in the Chinese exclusion case.

NOTES

1. John S. Saloma III, *Congress and the New Politics* (Boston: Little, Brown, 1969), pp. 21–22.

2. Louis W. Koenig, "More Power to the President (Not Less)," *New York Times Magazine,* January 3, 1965, p. 7.

3. William J. Keefe, *Congress and the American People* (Englewood Cliffs, N.J.: Prentice-Hall, 1980), p. 164.

4. Edward S. Corwin, *The Constitution and what it means today,* 12th ed. (Princeton: Princeton University Press, 1958), p. 187.

5. J. W. Peltason, *Corwin & Peltason's Understanding the Constitution,* 9th ed. (New York: Holt, Rinehart and Winston, 1982), p. 116.

6. *The Federalist Papers—Hamilton—Madison—Jay* (New York: New American Library, 1961), p. 224.

7. Ibid., pp. 228, 231.

8. Winton U. Solberg, *The Federal Convention and the Formation of the American States* (Indianapolis: Bobbs-Merrill, 1958), pp. 63–64.

9. *Notes of Debates in the Federal Convention of 1787 Reported by James Madison* (New York: Norton, 1966), pp. 27–34 (hereafter cited as *Madison's Notes*).

10. See the section entitled "The Conflicts on Representation" in Chapter 3.

11. See Chapter 4.

12. *Madison's Notes,* p. 362.

13. See the section entitled "Double Emergence of the Presidency" in Chapter 4.

14. Alfred H. Kelly and Winfred A. Harbison, *The American Constitution: Its Origins and Development,* 4th ed. (New York: Norton, 1970), p. 879; *Youngstown Co. v. Sawyer,* 343 U.S. 579.

15. "From a constitutional point of view, the most extraordinary fact about the seizure order was its total lack of statutory authority." Kelly and Harbison, *American Constitution,* p. 880.

16. *Youngstown Co. v. Sawyer,* p. 586.

17. Ibid., p. 585.

18. Ibid., p. 587.

19. Ibid., p. 633.

20. Ibid., pp. 635–38.

21. Ibid., pp. 638–39.

22. *Dames & Moore v. Regan,* 453 U.S. 654.

23. Ibid., p. 674.

24. Ibid., p. 680.

25. Ibid., p. 681.

26. *Vallandigham, Ex. parte,* 1 Wallace 243 (1864).

27. *Milligan, Ex parte,* 4 Wallace 2 (1866).

28. Kelly and Harbison, *American Constitution,* p. 840.

29. Wilfred E. Binkley, *President and Congress* (New York: Knopf, 1947), p. 111.

30. Ibid., pp. 111–12.

31. Ibid., pp. 112–13.

32. *Prize Cases,* 2 Black 635 (1863).

33. Ibid.

34. *Orlando v. Laird; Berk v. Laird,* 443 F. 2d. 1039 (1971).

35. Ibid., p. 1042.

36. Ibid.

37. Ibid., pp. 1042–43.

38. Ibid., p. 1043.

39. *Chae Chan Ping, In re,* 130 U.S. 581.

40. Ibid., p. 600.

41. *Edye v. Robertson,* 112 U.S. 580 (1884). "We are of the opinion that, so far as the provisions in that Act [of Congress] may be found to be in conflict with any treaty with a foreign nation they must prevail in all the judicial courts of this country." Ibid., p. 597.

PART III

THE PRESENT STATE OF
THE CONSTITUTIONAL SYSTEM

THE POTENTIALS OF THE REPRESENTATIONAL PYRAMID

The third and final portion of this study of the separate group character of the House of Representatives, the Senate, and the presidency will endeavor to identify contemporary aims and problems. We will be concerned with the enlarged scope of the constitutional system as well as with the common responsibilities of these three elected institutions in the realms of legislation, execution, and representation, and the difficulties that hinder the attainment of the purposes of the group.

Throughout Parts I and II of this book, various differences between this group of elected officials and the vast bureaucracies of appointed officials have been explained. The presidency and the houses of Congress form the public policy superstructure of the national government. Their primary duties are to integrate the policy differences among the different electoral messages and also among the several units of the legislative and executive systems.

Part III will begin with an analysis of the key aspects of the elected institutions. This will include the common functions and the separate structures. Then it will explain the special situation arising from the Supreme Court's continuing practice of not considering many issues of foreign and military policy. That places the group of elected institutions in an exposed position because on such matters there is no legitimating guidance by the judiciary.

Next, the three levels of constitutional separation in the national government will be explained in some detail. As noted earlier, this is inspired in part by the three levels of political liberty in Montesquieu's *The Spirit of the Laws*. This theory of constitutional arrangement assumes that checks and balances are a general end purpose and that the different patterns of separation are means to that end purpose.

Chapter 14 will examine the shared powers of the three elected institutions and their common duty to reconcile the various conflicts among the people and the government. The analysis will stress the interdependence of these institutions in the making of high-level public policy in both domestic and external relations.

12

Key Aspects of
the Elected Institutions

Congress represents the rich diversity of American life, the President
its necessary unity. . . . We need a strong President and a strong
Congress. The two are not incompatible but mutually reinforcing
through their representation of valid constituencies—the President
the nation, and the congressional houses the locality, state and
region. Both the national and local sectors of political society must
be rallied behind major policy. Accordingly, neither Congress nor
the President can have a monopoly of wisdom and an exclusive claim
to the exercise of leadership. What we seek is an effective cooperation between the two branches, with each a positive, constructive
participant.

Louis W. Koenig[1]

There is no basis for distinguishing the President from the Congress
if one considers the processes of government in which they participate, but a solid basis for distinction can be found in the roles they
play in these processes. The Executive's [the President's] role is
leadership—to initiate and impel; the Congress's, control—to over-
see and to approve, reject or amend.

Arthur Maass[2]

This book has focused on the group purpose of the House of
Representatives, the Senate, and the presidency. The most fundamental aspect that they have in common is that each is elected by
popular vote. But that also makes them deeply separated because

each institution receives a separate electoral message and the messages tend to differ in varying degrees. That situation presents this question: Does the political separation of these institutions provide sufficient check and balance to prevent undue concentration of power without functional separation?

Their electoral separations override the legal separations by which they are identified in the Constitution.[3] Moreover, they have fused their separate functions so that now they have common responsibilities for legislation, execution, and representation.[4]

This chapter will examine their common duties and the difficulties that they encounter in trying to achieve their common purpose. The last section, entitled "The Heavy Burden of Multiple Separations," explains the disunities in the individual institutions and the group. But it is directed also at the application of the legislative/ executive functional separation on top of the deeply political separation of the elected institutions.

THE COMMON FUNCTIONS AND RESPONSIBILITIES

To keep our bearings in this effort to explain a more positive perception of the houses of Congress and the presidency, it is necessary to keep in mind the primary obstacle in this endeavor. That is the strong tendency to associate Congress with legislation and the president with execution.[5] We have seen that these reflect the facade of the document but neither its inner structure nor the developments of 200 years. This study has shown from various angles that both institutions have become responsible for both functions.

Still more, the foremost change has been that now all three institutions are elected by the people, and this has elevated the group above the merely governmental functions. Each is a representational institution, and as a group they constitute a public policy superstructure. It has levels of rights and duties, with primary responsibility for the reconciliation of the differences arising from the electoral process and for the integration of public interest conflicts.

The common responsibility of Congress and the presidency applies to foreign as well as domestic policy, as previously noted. Chapter 5 reviewed the considerable extent to which the Constitution authorizes Congress to legislate with respect to external sovereignty. Chapter 7, on the establishment of the constitutional system, described the nature and scope of the acts of Congress concerning military affairs during the presidency of George Washington.

The policies of the Supreme Court seem to support cooperation between Congress and the presidency. Chapters 7 and 8 showed that the Court has favored delegation of policy-making discretion to the president and the executive departments.[6] As noted, the Supreme Court refused to decide the constitutionality of an act of Congress in advance of the actual execution of the law. Likewise, Chapters 10 and 11 noted that the Court strongly supported the delegation by Congress of presidential action in a South American war situation and disapproved of action by the president, without congressional authorization, to seize strike-bound steel mills during the Korean War.

The rights and duties of representational institutions, alone or as a group, are not specified in the Constitution. Chapter 1 identified the principal duties, and that classification is particularly pertinent at this point.

There are two general levels of such functions. The higher group concerns public relations, and the other involves government affairs. The responsibilities to the public include the reconciliation of their separate electoral positions, the integration of public interest conflicts, and the development of national objectives with respect to legislation and legitimation. The responsibilities in relation to the government include the integration of public policy conflicts, the development of legislative programs, the final action on proposed legislation, and general supervision of the legislative and executive systems.

THE INSTITUTIONAL SEPARATIONS

This book asserts that the three elected institutions have a special pattern of checks and balances because their political and institutional separations are sufficiently deep and strong to prevent undue concentration of power.[7] Those separations come with their election. Each elected institution receives a separate message from the voters of the nation. In addition, each house of Congress has another check or balance in the majority and minority party organizations. There is also the difference between the two-party structure of each house and the single party organization of the executive office of the president.[8]

Despite the existence of inner and outer forces of separation, there has been since the start of our constitutional system a continuing tendency to fuse the functions of legislation and execution so that, at least in the noncriminal law areas, there is an expanding area of common or shared functions among the houses of Congress and the presidency. The principle of "separated institutions sharing powers" seems to be increasingly applicable to the three elected institutions.

Chapters 8 and 9, on the changing priorities of both Congress and the presidency, explained that increasing diversity and competitiveness of the states, the representative districts, and the special interest groups have resulted in more demand for specialized laws and also increased the difficulty of enacting them.

The threefold character of the electoral system permits voters to split their ticket and to vote for a presidential candidate of one party and for a member of Congress of the other party. During the 56 years ending in 1987, the party identities of the elected institutions were:[9]

Institution	Republican	Democratic
President	22 years	34 years
Senate	10 years	46 years
House	4 years	52 years

Thus split ticket voting accentuates the institutional separation of the elected officials. The impact affects the parties differently. The Democratic presidents have had a Democratic Congress for all except two years (1947-49), while the Republican presidents have had one or both houses Democratic for all except two years (1953-55).

This has not been as advantageous to Democratic presidents as it may appear. The conservative bent of many southern Democrats has stymied Democratic presidents a good deal of the time. In fact, they have had congressional support in force only during the years 1933-36 and 1964-66.[10]

The triple-electoral system in the United States means that each elected institution receives a separate electoral verdict. When a house of Congress is perceived collectively, it is national in scope. Thus the system gives us three national electoral messages on top of other separations.

Often it is said that the president represents the entire nation, that a senator represents only a state, and that a member of the

House represents only a district. However, each house, as a collective, represents the entire nation. This is noted by Nelson W. Polsby, a leading analyst of the national elections:

> Now it is true that the President is elected on a nationwide basis and congressmen and senators individually are not, but congressmen and senators are in concert; collectively, they are elected on a national basis. . . . who knows why men are elected to public office; . . . it is perfectly possible for a candidate to be elected by a majority which disagrees with *all* his policy preferences. It is also perfectly possible for a particular electorate to elect a President, a senator, and a congressman, none of whom agree with one another to a significant extent about any public policies. And so an attempt to justify particular policies advocated by congressmen or Presidents based on their supposed link to the electorate seems dubious.[11]

Many persons may think in terms of individual officials rather than in terms of collective institutions. This is an area where those trained in survey research, attitude polls, and computer programming may be able to develop a way to formulate the electoral position of an institution and perhaps the compound position of the three institutions as the representational branch.[12]

There may be a further problem with respect to the Senate. Does it represent people or states? Each state has two senators regardless of the number of voters. The possible disproportion between senators and voters in the two parties is illustrated by the results in the 1980 elections. The voters chose 22 Republicans and 12 Democrats for the Senate. But the total popular vote for all Republican candidates for the Senate seats was 3 million votes less than the total popular vote for all Democratic candidates for the Senate.[13] The difference arose mostly from the vote in California and Ohio. In each, the Democratic candidate outpolled the Republican opponent by more than 1.5 million votes.[14]

The differences in the three electoral messages are evident in the varying percentages of the total vote received in the 1980 election:[15]

Office	Republicans	Democrats
Presidential	50.8%	41.0%
Senatorial	48.0	50.4
Congressional	46.0	51.0

What did the election decide with respect to the programs of the two parties? The voters seem to have preferred the Republican presidential policies and also the Democratic congressional policies. But those two sets of policies differ substantially.[16] This would seem to add to the political separation of the three elected representational institutions.

FINAL DETERMINATION OF NONJURIDICAL ISSUES

There appears to be a common assumption that the national government consists of three separate powers—Congress, president, and Supreme Court—and that each one may act upon any major issue. Here again, a common assumption may be too broad.

The houses of Congress and the presidency as a group seem to have a special burden in this regard. The Supreme Court does not decide certain types of issues. As a consequence, Congress and the president, if they agree, have the final determination on those questions. They are free of judicial review to the extent that the Court determines the issue nonjuridical.

The Constitution grants the Supreme Court and other courts established under Article III the authority to decide "cases or controversies." What meets that test is for the courts to decide, and the decision involves trained judgment. The judiciary has finality on "juridical issues," but only a professional lawyer may know what the term *juridical* means. The courts fortify their position of superior finality by refusing to decide nonjuridical issues. This began in England centuries ago.[17]

The Supreme Court's refusal to decide nonjuridical issues often has a disturbing element. Rather than explaining what a "nonjuridical" question is, which only a lawyer might understand, it calls the issue "political."[18] That may increase both the criticism and the confusion.

The leading precedent of the Supreme Court's refusal to decide foreign policy issues dealt with an 1804 grant of land by the government of Spain.[19] Its validity depended upon whether at that time a certain region had belonged to Spain or the United States. The opinion of Chief Justice John Marshall included this statement:

> If those departments which are intrusted with the foreign intercourse of the nation, which assert and maintain its interests against

foreign powers, have unequivocally asserted its right of dominion over a country of which it is in possession, and which it claims under a treaty; if the legislature has acted on the construction thus asserted, it is not in its own courts that this construction is to be denied. A question like this, respecting the boundaries of nations, is, as has been truly said, more a political than a legal question, and in its discussion, the courts of every country must respect the pronounced will of the legislature.[20]

Chief Justice Marshall indicated that both Congress and the president are responsible for national policy with respect to foreign affairs. The Supreme Court has refused certain other questions, such as whether the 1861 blockade of the southern states was legal,[21] whether a war had terminated,[22] whether the Alien Enemy Act of 1798 and the Alien Registration Act of 1948 gave the president authority to deport an alien,[23] and whether the Court should review orders of the Civil Aeronautics Board on foreign transportation that were subject to approval by the president.[24]

The most important issues of this character during recent years was the validity of the Vietnam War.[25] The Supreme Court did no more than refuse to hear decisions of a circuit court of appeals against servicemen who claimed that they had been wronged. One such opinion said that it could decide whether Congress had participated in the prosecution of the war. The Court stated "there was an abundance of continuing mutual participation in the prosecution of the war." The Court said that the political question doctrine prevented it from going beyond determining that there had been "some" mutual participation.[26] There had been no declaration of war, of course, but there had been appropriations and approving of conscription. The Court said "it is clear that the constitutional propriety of the means by which Congress has chosen to ratify and approve the protracted military operations in Southeast Asia is a political question."[27] This indicates that the Court considers congressional participation a necessity, but the Court seems eager to find participation.

The Supreme Court justices in 1962 changed their mind about one type of issue.[28] Formerly, the Court had refused to hear disputes concerning plans for apportionment of legislators. Its reversal may be due to the increased denigration of the individual right to vote. The moral factor may have overshadowed the public policy issues. The general limitation is not likely to go away. There is evidence that the practice goes back to at least 1460.[29]

The limitation is sometimes attributed to the doctrine of the separation of powers. But in one opinion the Supreme Court noted that the principle or practice "is equally well settled in England."[30]

Judges and political scientists may use the terms *juridical* and *political* in different ways. The judges seem to assume that *juridical* and *political* are mutually exclusive, while political scientists consider the judiciary to be political.

At the start, U.S. constitutional theory and practice may have considered judicial officers to differ basically from legislators and executives. There is definite evidence of this at the time the United States became independent and the new states undertook adopting constitutions. The leader in this was the state of Virginia. Its constitution set forth the doctrine of separate legislative, executive, and judicial departments, but its bill of rights included a provision that the first two should be separate from the judiciary and that there should be "frequent, certain, and regular elections" for the first two.[31]

In addition, Virginia had different terms for the two types of officials. Members of the House of Delegates had one-year terms, the Senators had staggered four-year terms, the governor was selected annually by the legislature, while the judges were appointed for good behavior. Massachusetts, also noted for its constitution, prescribed one-year terms for members of both houses of the legislature and for the governor, while judicial officers were appointed for good behavior.

Many of the Founders may have thought that the judiciary had a limited role in government, but now the self-restraint of the courts seems to cause criticism as well as confusion.

THE HEAVY BURDEN OF MULTIPLE SEPARATIONS

This study explains that the three elected institutions have sufficient institutional separation that functional separation is not needed to prevent undue concentration. Basic institutional separations result from the threefold character of the election process. The president, the Senate, and the House of Representatives often receive different messages from the voters, and they may continue to hold distinct public policy viewpoints.[32]

In addition to these deep-rooted political separations, there are several other factors that work against concentration of power both within particular branches and among the three elected institutions.

Prior analyses have indicated many causes of disunity in the houses of Congress and of increased need for the unifying and activating leadership of the president in order for Congress to be an effective operating force. The first decentralizing factor is that the membership of Congress has increased more than fivefold. Moreover, each of the 535 elected members is quite apt to have a distinct electoral constituency.[33]

The development of a committee system within each house is a further decentralizing force. Each house now has at least 20 major legislative committees and more than 100 subcommittees or special "select" committees. In fact, the power of the majority party may be in its committee chairmen, and the power of the minority party is apt to be in the ranking minority members of the various committees.

The outside influences also are diversified. "The particularistic and localistic nature of American democracy has created a particularistic and client serving administration" and an equally divided legislative system.[34] The specialized committees of each house are matched by specialized departments and agencies in the executive system and also by a complex pattern of special interest groups in the Washington lobbying community.

The inner organization—or disorganization—within each house is described by a former administrator:

> The conflict between Congress and the President, however, is not as difficult a problem as another conflict—especially difficult because it is not so obvious. That is the conflict between Congress and itself— between Congress as a whole and its own committees, and staffs. It is not obvious or apparent because Congress prefers, as an organized and disciplined entity, not to exist.
>
> It rather prefers to leave its undisciplined parts in control of pieces of its business. This process is not one of real delegation, because delegation implies accountability, and there is no effective way to hold the committees or staffs fully accountable to the whole Congress.[35]

Other scholarly analysts also have pointed out the decentralization within Congress. Years ago, Woodrow Wilson, then a professor, called the committees "the little legislatures of Congress." Now that designation is applied to the subcommittees.[36]

The decentralization and the spirit of disunity in Congress lead to one of the principal questions of this book. Are the houses of Congress able to provide adequate leadership themselves or do they need the policy-developing leadership of the president? A number of analysts on congressional-presidential relations provide these evaluations:

> The Congress is too numerous and too poorly organized to originate legislative programs, or to assume leadership functions.[37]

> An activist government requires strong legislative leadership. Under our system, the president can provide that leadership probably better than the Congress on many controversial, large-impact issues.[38]

> The dominance of the executive over Congress may be said to have developed as a consequence of the growing complexity of issues facing the national government.[39]

> The legislature is not the dominant influence in the legislative process. The President is more influential. He leads and Congress controls.[40]

The problems of presidential policy-making leadership of Congress involves not only the needs and wishes of the House and the Senate but also the attitude of the president. The factors that cause the president to be at a distance from the houses of Congress will be considered next.

Presidents differ politically in varying degrees from either or both houses of Congress. The election system is threefold, and there may be a president of one party and a Congress of the other. Moreover, parties are not monolithic. A president may differ from a Senate or House with a majority of the same party. A president may claim that only presidents are elected by the whole nation. But each house as a collective is elected by the entire nation. The Senate is elected by the voters in 50 states, and the House is chosen by voters in 435 districts. On the other hand, a president rarely receives more than 60 percent of the two-party vote. Yet most presidents claimed that they, and only they, are elected by and represent the entire nation. Moreover, the majority of U.S. citizens probably agree with that contention. Besides, there is a considerable tendency to agree with whomever is president.

There may be several other reasons for the separation of an incumbent president from the houses of Congress. Yet there is a general tendency to excuse presidential separation or independence as required by the doctrine of separate legislative, executive, and judicial powers.

Chapter 9 showed that presidents are not as much engaged in executive functions as they are intended to be by the separation doctrine. They are more likely to be involved in other functions, such as legislation or representation, while subordinate staffs of appointees carry on the executive operations.[41] The separation of a president from Congress is often due to differences in public policies. Yet presidents and many voters consider the separation justified under the doctrine of separate executive and legislative powers.

Some of the conflict between the president and Congress may result from the differences in the political party systems of the two institutions. Each house of Congress has both majority and minority party organizations. The two parties are continually face to face and organized to contest and accommodate.

The White House, on the other hand, has only a majority party organization. An incumbent president reaches office by a vote of about 60 percent. There is no executive branch structure for the minority presidential party as there is in the Congress for the minority senatorial and congressional parties. This would seem to accentuate the conflict between the president and Congress because that difference arose in part from the conflict between the presidential candidates.

There may be a number of extraconstitutional claims for presidential independence. One mentioned in Chapter 9 is the idea that the presidents have unqualified authority in matters affecting foreign and military actions. Chapter 11 showed that the Supreme Court disapproved of a presidential action during the Korean War where Congress had not approved the presidential procedure.

Some presidents, particularly Truman, Johnson, and Nixon, have fortified the claim of independence by the theory of a dynastic office. Like hereditary monarchs, they asserted that the office as received from their predecessors should be preserved so that it can be passed on intact to their successors. Johnson put the idea in these words:

At no time and in no way and for no reason can a President allow the integrity or the responsibility or the freedom of the office to be compromised or diluted or destroyed because when you destroy it, you destroy yourselves.

I hope and pray that by not allowing the Presidency to be involved in division and deep partisanship I shall be able to pass on to my successor a stronger office....[42]

Are presidents to think of themselves as dynastic monocrats, serving the presidential dynasty, rather than the nation? There may be times when there seems to be public support for such a contention. This raises the issue of a Congress-free president. Clearly, the Constitutional Convention did not intend this. Chapter 11 showed that the Supreme Court did not approve presidential independence even in a wartime situation.

Clearly, there is much more conflict or separation between Congress and the presidency than is needed to prevent undue concentration of power. There is little likelihood that either the president or Congress, or even the critics of one or both, will accept an unfamiliar constitutional theory, but the public may benefit from a concept that allows a more positive perception of the elected institutions.

The application of the doctrine of a "mixed constitution" or the pattern of separated institutions sharing functions would not only promote cooperation directly but also would eliminate the constitutional color for ideas of independence that are outside the doctrine of separate powers.

NOTES

1. Louis W. Koenig, *The Chief Executive*, 4th ed. (New York: Harcourt Brace Jovanovich, 1981), pp. 157, 181.

2. Arthur Maass, *Congress and the Common Good* (New York: Basic Books, 1983), p. 13.

3. See Chapters 4 and 5.

4. On the idea of separated institutions sharing powers, see Richard E. Neustadt, *Presidential Power: The Politics of Leadership* (New York: John Wiley, 1960), p. 33.

5. See Chapter 1.

6. Alfred H. Kelly and Winfred A. Harbison, *The American Constitution: Its Origins and Development*, 4th ed. (New York: Norton, 1970), pp. 649-54, 743-48.

7. See Chapters 1 and 13.

8. See the section entitled "Party Composition of the Representational Branch" in Chapter 7.

9. *Congressional Quarterly's Guide to Congress*, 3d ed. (Washington, D.C.: Congressional Quarterly Press, 1982), pp. 894–97; *Congressional Quarterly Weekly Report*, vol. 39, no. 17, April 25, 1981, pp. 717–25, especially p. 718 (California) and p. 723 (Ohio).

10. Nelson W. Polsby, *Congress and the Presidency* (Englewood Cliffs, N.J.: Prentice-Hall, 1965); Charles O. Jones, *The United States Congress: People, Place and Policy* (Homewood, Ill.: Dorsey Press, 1982), pp. 8–9, 234–35, 347, 442–43; William J. Keefe, *Congress and the American People* (Englewood Cliffs, N.J.: Prentice-Hall, 1980), pp. 103–20; Stephen J. Wayne, *The Legislative Presidency* (New York: Harper, 1978), pp. 8–24, 109–13.

11. Polsby, *Congress and the Presidency*, pp. 110–11.

12. An official accommodation might be obtained by a three-sided commission, with five members each appointed by the president, the majority leader of the Senate, and the Speaker of the House. Such a commission brought forth a nearly acceptable agenda to "rescue" the Social Security system. *New York Times*, December 17, 1981, p. B16.

13. *Congressional Quarterly's Guide to Congress*, pp. 894–97; *Congressional Quarterly Weekly Report*, vol. 39, no. 17, April 25, 1981; pp. 717–25.

14. *Congressional Quarterly Weekly Report*, vol. 39, no. 17, April 25, 1981, p. 718.

15. The total vote for the three types of candidates was:

	Democratic	Republican
President	35,483,820	43,901,812
House	38,951,337	37,059,354
Senate	29,889,954	27,002,538

Ibid., p. 713.

16. Mixed government may be cooperative or adversarial. "I know of no one who publicly advocates this particular pattern of institutional behavior [the adversarial mode]. But it has been characteristic of interbranch relations during periods in which different parties control the White House and the Congress." Jones, *United States Congress*, pp. 8–9.

17. Philippa Strumm, *The Supreme Court and "Political Questions": A Study in Judicial Evasion* (University: University of Alabama Press, 1974), pp. 9, 148; Page and Petracca, *The American Presidency* (New York: McGraw-Hill, 1983), pp. 298–99.

18. Edward S. Corwin, ed., *The Constitution of the United States of America: Analysis and Interpretation* (Washington, D.C.: Government Printing Office, 1953), p. 547.

19. *Foster v. Neilson*, 2 Peters 253 (1829), p. 308.

20. Ibid.

21. *The Prize Cases*, 2 Bl. 635 (1863).

22. *Commercial Trust v. Miller*, 262 U.S. 51 (1923).

23. *Ludecke v. Watkins*, 335 U.S. 160 (1948); *Harisiades v. Shaughnessy*, 342 U.S. 580 (1952).

24. *Chicago and Southern Air Lines v. Waterman Steamship Corp.,* 333 U.S. 103–18, at 111 (1948).

25. See Page and Petracca, *American Presidency,* p. 299.

26. *Orlando v. Laird,* 429 F. (2d) 302 (C.A.N.Y.) remand 317 F. Supp. 715, affirmed 443 F. (2d) 1039, cer. den. 92 Sup/Ct. 94, 404 U.S. 869, 306 L. Ed. (2d) 113, 443 F. (2d) 1042.

27. Ibid., p. 1043.

28. *Baker v. Carr,* 369 U.S. 186 (1962).

29. Strumm, *Supreme Court,* p. 148.

30. "Who is sovereign, *de jure* or *de facto,* of a territory is not a judicial, but a political, question, the determination of which by the legislative executive departments of any government conclusively binds the judges, as well as all other officers, citizens and subjects, of that government. This principle has always been upheld by this court, and has been affirmed under a great variety of circumstances. . . . It is equally well settled in England." *Henry Jones v. United States,* 137 U.S. 202, 212 (1890).

31. "The Virginia Bill of Rights," Art. 5. Henry S. Commager, ed., *Documents of American History,* 5th ed., vol. 1 (New York: Appleton-Century-Crofts, 1949), pp. 103–4.

32. See the earlier section "The Institutional Separation." Note the discussion of split-ticket voting during 1953–87.

33. Constituencies may have more impact than interest groups. "In particular, interest groups appear to have slight influence on congressmen's voting decisions unless the groups are connected with their constituencies in some fashion." John W. Kingdon, *Congressmen's Voting Decisions,* 2d ed. (New York: Harper & Row, 1981), p. 174.

34. James Q. Wilson, "The Rise of the Bureaucratic State," *The Public Interest,* 41 (Fall 1975): 103.

35. Don K. Price, *America's Unwritten Constitution* (Baton Rouge: Louisiana State University Press, 1983), p. 132.

36. Joseph P. Harris, *Congress and the Legislative Process,* 2d ed. (New York: McGraw-Hill, 1972), p. 3; George Goodwin, Jr., "Subcommittees: The Miniature Legislatures of Congress," *American Political Science Review* 56 (1962): 506–604; Morris P. Fiorina, *Congress: Keystone of the Washington Establishment* (New Haven: Yale University Press, 1977), p. 67.

37. C. Herman Pritchett, *The American Constitutional System* (New York: McGraw-Hill, 1981), pp. 31.

38. Wayne, *Legislative Presidency,* p. 24.

39. Jones, *United States Congress,* p. 6.

40. Maass, *Congress and the Common Good,* p. 10.

41. Wayne, *Legislative Presidency,* p. 24; George C. Edwards III, *Presidential Influence in Congress* (San Francisco: Freeman, 1980), pp. 5–6, 117; Arthur Maass, *Congress and the Common Good,* pp. 10–14. "The task of the President is no longer confined to executing the laws enacted by Congress; he must also provide leadership in legislation." George B. Galloway, *The Legislative Process in Congress* (New York: Crowell, 1953), p. 426. Gary Orfield, *Congressional Power: Congress and Social Change* (New York: Harcourt Brace Jovanovich, 1975), pp.

16-21; Charles O. Jones, *The United States Congress* (Homewood, Ill.: Dorsey Press, 1982), pp. 6-7. See the section entitled "Public Policy Interdependence" in Chapter 12.

42. Lyndon Johnson, "Comments on the Presidency," in Robert S. Hirschfield, ed., *The Power of the Presidency: Concepts and Controversy,* 3d ed. (New York: Aldine, 1982), p. 152.

13

Three Levels of Constitutional Separation

The time is long past when a student of politics could be content with the study only of legislatures, executives, and judiciaries. He is concerned with all the political structures to be found in a political system. . . . Particular functions are not specific to a particular structure; each political or governmental structure may perform a number of functions.

M. J. C. Vile[1]

In this day and age, the Constitution is a fallible and incomplete guide to national policy-making. Instead of three branches of government, each with its clearly defined sphere of competence and activity, there may be five branches of government in any particular area, or seven, or twenty, or only one. The number of "branches" involved varies from time to time and from issue to issue. And the roles these branches play may vary greatly too.

Nelson W. Polsby[2]

The doctrine of separate legislative, executive, and judicial powers has more concrete sources than the writings of Montesquieu,[3] but the U.S. reverence for the theory derives in large part from the idea attributed to him that liberal constitutionalism rests upon that separation of functions.[4] In fact, scholars of England and the United States make Montesquieu stand for the proposition that political liberty requires such a threefold separation.

More thorough examination of Montesquieu's principal work, *L'Esprit des Lois* (translated as *The Spirit of the Laws*), discloses that it presents three levels of constitutional distribution designed to protect three corresponding types of political liberty. Moreover, the highest level of institutional arrangement, which Montesquieu calls "the fundamental constitution," consists of two branches of the legislature and a veto-empowered executive. This is comparable to the English Parliament of Commons, Lords, and kings, as well as the United States' three elected institutions, the two houses of Congress and the presidency.

This chapter will review relevant portions of Montesquieu's principal work. The analyses will indicate the ways in which the common view of Montesquieu is an inadequate picture of his constitutional theory.

THE CONTRIBUTIONS OF MONTESQUIEU

Writers on governmental theory and practice have made Montesquieu stand for the idea that political liberty in a constitutional system requires the separation of legislative, executive, and judicial powers. Yet there are a number of ways in which that is misleading. First, Montesquieu identifies not one but three kinds of political liberty and three patterns of distribution. Second, the separation of the three powers named above concerns political liberty of the individual citizen. Third, that political liberty, he tells us, depends upon the goodness of the criminal laws. Fourth, political liberty with regard to the constitution seems to concern the political composition of the society. Fifth, that political liberty involves the "fundamental constitution," which consists of two legislative branches and the executive. Sixth, Montesquieu says that a government may be moderate when the legislative and executive powers are held by one person if the people possess the judicial power. Seventh, the third type of liberty concerns taxation and a mixed pattern of powers. Eighth, in all situations the legislation needs to be moderate and sociologically relevant.

The Spirit of the Laws was published in 1748 after 20 years of writing and rewriting.[5] American colonists began quoting it in 1762.[6] Most famous is an account of the political liberty in England, but that may have been a covert prescription to change the despotism in

France.[7] The book was deemed scholarly and scientific at the time, but it does not meet contemporary standards in such matters.

Most of the 31 chapterlike books of *The Spirit of the Laws* concern specific types of civil or political laws. Three books deal with political liberty. The titles of these books distinguish the three kinds of liberty:

> Book XI. Of the Laws which Establish Political Liberty with Regard to the Constitution.
> Book XII. Of the Laws that Form Political Liberty in Relation to the Subject [*Citoyen*].
> Book XIII. Of the Relation which the Levying of Taxes and the Greatness of the Public Revenues Bear to Liberty.

Montesquieu says that he will explain the first type in Book XI, but the first few chapters of that book discuss liberty in general, and its Chapter 4 provides the psychological basis of a broad principle of checks and balances:

> Democratic and aristocratic states are not in their own nature free. Political liberty is to be found only in moderate governments; and even in these it is not always found. It is there only when there is no abuse of power. But constant experience shows us that every man invested with power is apt to abuse it, and to carry his authority as far as it will go. Is it not strange, though true, to say that virtue itself has need of limits.
>
> To prevent this abuse, it is necessary from the very nature of things that power should be a check to power. A government may be so constituted, as no man shall be compelled to do things to which the law does not oblige him, nor forced to abstain from things which the law permits.[8]

Thus Montesquieu makes liberty relative to the laws, but this may be qualified by other ideas and proposals. He probably is talking about the political laws enacted by a democratic/aristocratic legislature, and elsewhere he imposes two limitations upon that legislature. It must follow the "general spirit of the national society," and that derives from such diverse, relevant causes as geography, manners, governmental precedents, laws, and religion.[9] Secondly, the legislature is to follow the spirit of moderation and avoid extremes.[10]

This is an example of the need for making explicit the conditions that Montesquieu leaves implicit.

The idea that power should be a check upon power provides us with the overriding principle of checks and balances. This is the end or purpose of the three levels of constitutional arrangement.

There are other apparent digressions in Book XI and even in its Chapter 6, which analyzes the Constitution of England in some 68 paragraphs. Montesquieu does not get to the institutional pattern that he believes will assure political liberty with regard to the constitution until paragraphs 55 and 56. These provide:

> Here, then, is the fundamental constitution of the government we are treating of. The legislative body being composed of two parts, they check one another by the mutual privilege of rejecting. They are both restrained by the executive power, as the executive is by the legislature.
>
> These three powers should naturally form a state of repose or inaction. But as there is a necessity for movement in the course of human affairs, they are forced to move, but still in concert.[11]

Thus the institutional pattern designed to assure political liberty with regard to the constitution embodies the two branches of the legislature, which are democratic and aristocratic in character, and the executive monarchy, but not the judiciary. This resembles the classical concept of the "mixed constitution." It brings together the monarchical, aristocratic, and democratic forces of a politically mixed society.[12] There are similar findings by the three professors who have made the most scholarly analyses of the doctrine of the separation of powers and its origins.[13]

Montesquieu most likely was influenced by the English Parliament of the 1720s when he visited London. He states in Paragraph 65 that he is interested in the laws rather than the practices. That may mean that he was purposely disregarding the political practices of Sir Robert Walpole, the king's first minister. It may also mean that his prescription for France was based upon the laws and not upon the tactics that led to the English parliament-cabinet system.[14]

The common belief is that Montesquieu proposed only one pattern, which embodies separation of legislative, executive, and judicial powers. We will see that this relates to the second kind of political liberty, that relating to the liberty of the individual subject or citizen. Montesquieu's ideas on that can be gleaned from Book XII. Its first two chapters include the following:

> It is not sufficient to have treated of political liberty in relation to the constitution; we must examine it likewise in the relation it bears to the subject. . . .
>
> The constitution may happen to be free, and the subject not. The subject may be free, and not the constitution. In those cases, the constitution will be free by right, and not in fact; the subject will be free in fact, and not by right. . . .

2. Of the Liberty of the Subject

> Philosophic liberty consists in the free exercise of the will; or at least, if we must speak agreeably to all systems, in an opinion that we have the free exercise of our will. Political liberty consists in security, or, at least, in the opinion that we enjoy security.
>
> This security is never more dangerously attacked than in public or private accusations. It is, therefore, on the goodness of criminal laws that the liberty of the subject principally depends. . . .

Montesquieu also notes that this liberty does not depend entirely upon the quality of the laws; it rests also upon the knowledge and practice in criminal trials and judgments.[15]

The institutional pattern that will assure the political liberty in relation to the subject is not stated here in Book XII. In fact, it had already been set forth. Paragraphs 3 to 7 of the chapter on the English Constitution in Book XI states:

> [3] The political liberty of the subject is a tranquillity of mind arising from the opinion each person has of his safety. In order to have this liberty, it is requisite the government be so constituted as one man need not be afraid of another.
>
> [4] When the legislative and executive powers are united in the same person, or in the same body of magistrates, there can be no liberty; because apprehensions may arise, lest the same monarch or senate should enact tyrannical laws, to execute them in a tyrannical manner.
>
> [5] Again, there is no liberty, if the judiciary power be not separated from the legislative and executive. Were it joined with the legislative, the life and liberty of the subject would be exposed to arbitrary control; for the judge would be then the legislator. Were it joined to the executive power, the judge might behave with violence and oppression.

[6] There would be an end of everything, were the same man or the same body, whether of the nobles or of the people, to exercise those three powers, that of enacting laws, that of executing the public relations, and of trying the causes of individuals.

[7] Most kingdoms in Europe enjoy a moderate government because the prince who is invested with the two first powers leaves the third to his subjects. . . .[16]

When analysts of U.S. government wish to show the contribution of Montesquieu to our constitutional system of distributed powers, they are most likely to call attention to Paragraphs 4, 5, and 6 of the above quoted excerpts. Quite often, these three paragraphs are quoted with little or no consideration of what appears before and after, even though that may be quoting without regard to context. Careful attention to Paragraph 3 would seem to be most needed because it precedes Paragraphs 4, 5, and 6, which are highly rated, and also because it tells us that the matter at hand is political liberty in relation to the subject.[17]

Logically, Montesquieu is saying that what is immediately following Paragraph 3 concerns the liberty of the subject. This conclusion is supported by the fact that Paragraph 3 associates this kind of liberty with "the opinion each person has of his safety" and Paragraph 4 deals with "apprehensions" about tyrannical actions by officials. Also, Paragraph 5 refers to "the life and liberty of the subject."

Montesquieu may overstate the scope of necessary separation. Paragraph 6 seems to be superfluous. It says that liberty is lacking if all three powers are in the same hands even though Paragraphs 4 and 5 state that there would be no liberty if any two of the three powers are in the same person or group. Paragraph 7 also tends to undercut these warnings because it says that there can be moderate government when the first two powers are in the same hands, if the third power is in the people.

When *The Spirit of the Laws,* and particularly the chapter on the Constitution of England is examined closely, it is evident: (1) that Montesquieu makes a basic distinction between the liberty of the constitution and the liberty of the subject; (2) that the first aims to protect the mixed political society and the second seeks to protect the legal integrity of the individual; (3) that the one involves a "fundamental constitution" composed of three institutions, that is, the two branches of the legislature and the executive, while the second entails the sequence of legislative, executive, and judicial functions; and (4) that the judiciary is not a part of the first arrangement but is the most important element of the second.

Montesquieu seems especially confusing because he explains both of these types of political liberty in the chapter on the English system even though that analysis of England is supposed to concern only "liberty with regard to the constitution."[18]

In Montesquieu's work a basic distinction is made between these two kinds of liberty and power arrangement. That difference is also applicable to the Constitution of the United States and our democratic republic. The citizenry has two great safeguards in the constitutional system. One is the tripartite system of representation, and the other is the compound guarantee of individual rights in the several amendments. Next, these patterns of separation will be examined under the titles of the public policy superstructure and the criminal law infrastructure.

THE PUBLIC POLICY SUPERSTRUCTURE

Chapter 1, in explaining that the aim of this book is to identify the group character of the two houses of Congress and the presidency, called those three institutions the public policy superstructure of the U.S. national government.[19] That term is appropriate in this analysis of Montesquieu because it fits his idea of the "fundamental constitution." He defined that to consist of two branches of the legislature—the people's representatives and a body of nobles—and the veto-empowered executive. Montesquieu probably was describing in general the 1700 English Parliament of Commons, Lords, and king.[20] Each of the three concerns legislation and, perhaps, representation.

The U.S. public policy superstructure may resemble in general structure the Parliament of 1700, but it is not comparable to the contemporary British system. England has developed a party-cabinet system in which the ministers are members of the majority party in the Parliament.[21] Now the king and the House of Lords are formal so that only the Commons is sovereign.

Some U.S. observers admire the British system for its inner harmony and suggest that this country adopt the English system. But the United States has three elected institutions and a much looser party system. A Congress-related cabinet most likely would not function as the English system does. Also, it might divert attention from the fundamental fact that here there are three electoral positions whereas in England there is only one. It might be better if the conflict remained open and sharply visible because what most needs adjustment may be the independent attitude of the presidents and the representatives.

The principal responsibilities and functions of the public policy superstructure will be explained below.

Composite Constituency Representation. Each house of Congress, viewed collectively, and the president are elected by the voters of the nation, and each receives a separate electoral message. If there is to be a single set of public policies to guide the nation and the government, the primary task for the elected institutions is to ascertain a composite electoral message. That is probably the highest application of the idea of separated institutions sharing common functions.

Montesquieu recognized that in times of necessity the three institutions would need to act in concert. This indicates that he regarded separation in this situation to be preliminary to a necessary accommodation. They are separated institutionally and politically so that there are checks and balances without functional separation.

Official Public Communication. The citizenry of the nation is dependent upon adequate and accurate information about the government and its relations with the people. The president now dominates the public relations of the government: he may bring some unity to the vast outpouring of information. A more organized, composite system of public information might be helpful.

High-Level Integration of Public Conflicts. This may be the supreme function for the public policy superstructure. The United States deeply considers itself a democratic society and one with a strong emphasis upon individualism. In this country there is a high degree of conflict on the meaning of the "public interest" in many situations. Professor Andrew Hacker states, "Whether we like it or not, a society which encourages the full flowering of individual liberty is, and can only be, a stratified society."[22] Professor Murray Edelman points out that the political scene is "a pattern of ongoing events that spells threat or reassurance" and that it has the following multiplicity: "For everyone the political scene is a pastische of several patterns, but always there are threatening ones. That one man's reassurance is another's threat guarantees that threat will always be present for all men."[23] Moreover, the differences are often ideological; they are almost polar positions, which are held firmly and asserted sharply.

A political society functions better if there are few wide differences and more or less common public positions. Conflicts need to be resolved in substantial degree, and the forces best situated for that purpose are the elected officials in their institutional capacity. The public may need to pay less attention to the media drama among the two houses of Congress and the president and look more for composite reconciliations of the electoral conflicts.

Composite Guidance of the Middle Structures. Imprecise ideas about the separation of powers may be responsible for much of the widespread bewilderment at the "many-splintered" executive branch of the national government. "The conflict between president and Congress over authority to superintend the departments has never been settled."[24] Congress and the president struggle against each other for the control of the administration "but bureaucracy escapes."[25]

Constitutional ambiguity may be one major cause of this difficulty, but even more important is the fact that specialized members of the legislative and fiscal committees of Congress often have more experience and knowledge than the presidential appointees in the corresponding departments. For instance, assistant departmental secretaries have average tenure of less than three years, while senior members of congressional committees may have eight or a dozen years experience. This has sharp consequences. Career bureaucrats tend to align with members of Congress because they stay long and can do more for cooperative executives.[26]

Presidents may dominate the few executive matters that get into the headlines, but those are not likely to be representative of the total activity of the executive branch. The incidents that are publicized may be true in fact, but they are probably not representative. Neither the public media nor the media public seems to be interested in most of the administrative activity and its management. Most of it may be too dull to be news.

THE CRIMINAL LAW INFRASTRUCTURE

The peculiar essence of sovereign national government is the rightful use of extreme coercion to enforce laws and rules of taxation and regulation against individuals within the jurisdiction of the political community.[27]

The Confederation of the United States of America, which for the years 1781–87 preceded our constitutional system, did not have such authority. All such power was in the states. The Confederation Congress could not function successfully even in foreign affairs because of its inability to enforce obligations against individuals. The Confederation endeavored to function on the basis of assessment against the states, but the states were not sufficiently obliging.

The Constitution of 1787, as noted, nationalized a substantial portion of the internal sovereignty of the United States. As a result the central government was then able to operate more effectively in both foreign and domestic matters.

The superstructure, described in the preceding section, is a pyramid of institutions. The criminal law infrastructure is a sequence of functions. The superstructure is a political arrangement; the infrastructure is a legal one. It is a sequence of legislative, executive, and judicial functions with respect to a sovereign statute. It may be comparatively rigid in its order, a quality that had its origin in the protests and revolts of seventeenth century England.

The English criminal jurisprudence has a long tradition of separating application from legislation. The order of executive and judicial action may differ. Locke's *Treatise on Government* at one point places execution after adjudication.[28] There, execution is the enforcement of the judicial decree rather than that of the legislated statute. It may highlight the dependence of the judge upon others for enforcement. It also indicates that "execution" relates to the enforcement of prior actions of the legislature or the judiciary or both.

The sequence of legislative, executive, and judicial functions was the essence of Montesquieu's statement about political liberty of the individual citizen. As noted earlier in this chapter, Montesquieu asserted that political liberty depended upon the goodness of the criminal laws. The relation of the legislative-executive-judicial sequence to the English criminal law is noted by the leading analysts of the separation of powers.[29]

The American colonists became deeply interested in proper criminal law procedure about 1762, when the English began to use stern methods to enforce tax laws and trade regulations in the hopes of raising new revenues. The first use of Montesquieu's ideas in protesting English methods, reported in Paul Spurlin's book *Montesquieu in America,* was in 1762. That instance was a letter by James Otis to the editor of the *Boston Gazette.* The proclamations issued by Congresses during 1765, 1774, and 1776 protested the failure of the English to abide by proper procedure.[30]

THE MIXED POWER MIDDLE STRUCTURE

This volume recognizes that the general U.S. concept of separation of powers—the separation of legislative, executive, and judicial powers—applies to the vast middle structure of U.S. national government. In fact, there are only two quite limited exceptions. One is for the high-level public policy making of the elected members of the houses of Congress and the presidency. The other is for the appointed officials engaged in the criminal law process, which also is limited. Between these two is most of the governmental operation. It will be referred to here as mixed power middle structure. Here there is flexible mixture of legislative, executive, and judicial functions. This vast middle area will be analyzed and explained because its nature and operation affect considerably the operation of the three elected institutions in the public policy superstructure.

The mixed power middle structure is assumed to consist of four sublevels: specialized committees of the houses of Congress, secretaries of the executive departments, changing political executives, and continuing administrative career personnel. These divisions are not official, and the names we use for them are not commonly used. But they entail elements that make for separation and check and balance within the area. Each of the sublevels will be elaborated upon in the ensuing discussion.

The foremost attribute of the whole middle structure is the specialization of endeavor, such as that of the legislative committees of Congress and the executive departments and agencies. The specialization provides some separation and lessens the danger of concentration of authority.

The highest sublevel consists of the leaders of the specialized committees of Congress, distinct from the central leaders, such as the Speaker and the vice-president, and the majority and minority leaders. It excludes such central entities as the rules committees. It includes professional and technical actions as members of the specialized committees, such as the armed services, finance, and agriculture, and the staffs of such groups.

The second highest branch, that is, the departmental secretaries, consists of the secretaries and general undersecretaries of the departments of the executive branch. This includes the members of the president's cabinet as individual executives.

The two top sublevels are comparable in scope and interest. One may be legally legislative and the other legally executive, but they have similar governmental specialties, which tends to bring them together and to cause a considerable fusion of legislation and execution. They are not connected by any structural bridge, official or unofficial, as there is in the English cabinet system, so that much of their separate and joint success depends upon the mutual disposition to work together. That, in fact, may be the key to achievement in the whole U.S. system.

The third and fourth sublevels are the major divisions of the national bureaucracy. The changing political executives sublevel is at least officially the higher group. There may be only 10,000 in this group. The continuing administrative career personnel sublevel may number more than 2.5 million. The great hidden problem of the national administration lies in the fact that the higher group is political and changing while the lower group is career and continuing. At times, and probably many times, the lower and more experienced force may have its way against the higher one.

The changing political executives are largely appointees of the president or the president's top executives, such as departmental secretaries or the heads of large agencies. These appointments are usually made for policy or even political reasons. Such officials are selected presumably to carry out the policies of the president at the time.

This group includes the specialized undersecretaries and assistant secretaries, agency and bureau chiefs, a portion of the senior civil service, and their various aides and assistants. They endeavor to manage the vast career bureaucracy. There is a wholesale change of "political executives" when the White House shifts from one party to the other. But there is also much change during a presidential reign because many are outsiders whose lifetime occupational interests are in business, education, or other professional areas. Their short tenure increases the difficulties of managing the vast career bureaucracy.

NOTES

1. M. J. C. Vile, *Constitutionalism and the Separation of Powers* (Oxford: Clarendon Press, 1967), pp. 290–91.

2. Nelson W. Polsby, *Congress and the Presidency,* 3d ed. (Englewood Cliffs, N.J.: Prentice-Hall, 1976), p. 4.

3. Baron de Montesquieu, *The Spirit of the Laws,* vol. 1 (New York: Hafner, 1949), pp. 149–220; Roger Caillois, *Oeuvres Completes de Montesquieu,* vol. 2 (Paris, 1951), pp. 393–473.

4. In *The Federalist No. 47* Madison refers to "the political maxim that the legislative, executive and judiciary departments ought to be separate and distinct" and later says that the "oracle who is always consulted and cited on this subject is the celebrated Montesquieu." *The Federalist* (New York: Modern Library), pp. 312–13. George Sabine, *The History of Political Theory,* 3d ed. (New York: Holt, Rinehart and Winston, 1961), pp. 551–60; Vile, *Separation of Powers,* pp. 85–86.

5. Robert Shackleton, *Montesquieu: A Critical Biography* (Oxford: Oxford University Press, 1961), pp. 225–377; Emile Durkheim, *Montesquieu and Rousseau: Forerunners of Sociology* (Ann Arbor: University of Michigan Press, 1960); John Plamenatz, *Man and Society,* vol. 1 (New York: McGraw Hill, 1963), pp. 253–98; Melvin Richter, *The Political Theory of Montesquieu* (Cambridge: Cambridge University Press, 1977).

6. Paul Merrill Spurlin, *Montesquieu in America 1760–1801* (University: Louisiana State University Press, 1940), p. 99.

7. Montesquieu "addressed himself to the situation then existing in France. Louis XV's despotism was becoming more and more oppressive." Alpheus T. Mason and Richard H. Leach, *In Quest of Freedom: American Political Thought and Practice* (Englewood Cliffs, N.J.: Prentice-Hall, 1959), p. 24. "Montesquieu unquestionably was concerned with preserving the privileges of the nobility as an intermediary body of the realm." Raymond Aron, *Main Currents in Sociological Thought: I: Montesquieu/Comte/Marx/Tocqueville* (New York: Basic Books, 1965), p. 53. C. E. Vaughan, *Studies in the History of Political Philosophy Before and After Rousseau,* vol. 1 (New York: Russell & Russell, 1960), pp. 253–302; Richter, *Political Theory of Montesquieu,* pp. 5–8.

8. Montesquieu, *Spirit of the Laws,* vol. 1, p. 150.

9. Ibid., vol. 1, pp. 293–94.

10. Ibid., vol. 2, p. 156.

11. Ibid., vol. 1, p. 160

12. See Chapter 2.

13. Vile, *Separation of Powers*, pp. 35–37; Francis D. Wormuth, *The Origins of Modern Constitutionalism* (New York: Harper & Bros., 1949), pp. 7, 19, 30, 130, 136; W. B. Gwyn, *The Meaning of Separation of Powers* (New Orleans: Tulane University Press, 1965), pp. 24–27.

14. Vile, *Separation of Powers*, pp. 70–75; Shackleton, *Montesquieu*, pp. 291–301; Plamenatz, *Man and Society*, pp. 282–98.

15. Montesquieu, *Spirit of the Laws*, vol. 1, pp. 183–88.

16. Ibid., vol. 1, pp. 151–52.

17. See, for instance, Sir W. Ivor Jennings, *The Law and the Constitution*, 3d ed. (London: University of London Press, 1943), pp. 18–30. Sir Ivor quotes verbatim Paragraphs 4, 5, and 6 of the chapter on the English Constitution; he describes the first two paragraphs, which refer to three "powers" that seem to be the three kinds of positive law—the law of nations, the civil law, and the political law. But he does not quote or mention the third paragraph, which indicates that the subject is the liberty of the individual subject or citizen. He does not note that Book XII says that such liberty depends upon "the goodness of the criminal laws." Nor does he refer to Paragraph 7, which shows the importance of judicial power even though Paragraph 32 says that judicial power is next to nothing. Jennings says that "democracy" keeps Britain free, but he does not mention Montesquieu's "fundamental constitution," which includes democratic representation.

18. See bk. XI, chap. 1, Montesquieu, *Spirit of the Laws*, vol. 1, p. 149.

19. See Chapters 1 and 12.

20. See Chapter 2.

21. See Sir Ivor Jennings, *Cabinet Government*, 2d ed. (Cambridge: University Press, 1951); Richard Rose, *Politics in England* (Boston: Little, Brown, 1964), pp. 91, 103–23, 189–207.

22. Andrew Hacker, "Liberal Democracy and Social Control," in Edward Keynes and David Adamany, eds., *The Borzoi Reader in American Politics* (New York: Alfred Knopf, 1971), p. 116.

23. Murray Edelman, *The Symbolic Uses of Politics* (Urbana: University of Illinois Press, 1964), p. 13.

24. Richard M. Pious, *The American Presidency* (New York: Basic Books, 1979), p. 213.

25. Charles M. Hardin, *Presidential Power and Accountability* (Chicago: University of Chicago Press, 1974), p. 15.

26. See, in general, Hugh Heclo, *A Government of Strangers: Executive Politics in Washington* (Washington, D.C.: Brookings Institution, 1977).

27. See the section entitled "Functional Interdependence of Criminal Law Process" in Chapter 2; see also Chapter 3 and "Statutory Foundation of the National Infrastructure" in Chapter 7.

28. Peter Laslett, ed., *Locke's Two Treatises of Government* (Cambridge: University Press, 1960), p. 369 (chap. IX, par. 125).

29. Wormuth, *Modern Constitutionalism*, pp. 59–70; Gwyn, *Separation of Powers*, pp. 28–65; Vile, *Separation of Powers*, pp. 39–51.

30. See Spurlin, *Montesquieu in America*, p. 99.

14

Group Character of the Elected Institutions

The people elect the president, but they are not organized to support him in office: it is to Congress that he must constantly turn for the fulfillment of his objectives.

Pendleton Herring[1]

In a constitutional system compounded of diversity and antagonism, the Presidency looms up as the countervailing force of unity and harmony.

Clinton Rossiter[2]

But assigning the president a unique position is not the same as giving the president a mandate to govern. Even with the backing of a massive electoral majority, the president is not in charge. The president's job in the constitutional system is not to lead a followership; it is to elicit leadership from the other institutions of self-government and help make that leadership effective.

Hugh Heclo[3]

This final chapter will concern the problems of perceiving a more positive group character for the House of Representatives, the Senate, and the presidency. The first obstacle, as shown repeatedly, is the almost instinctive assumption of most people that Congress is simply legislative and the president is simply executive.

The new perception starts with the idea that these elected institutions are a separate group apart from and above all appointed officials and employees of the legislative and executive systems. We have called this group the public policy superstructure and explained that its checks and balances come from the political separation of the institutions and not the legal separation of the functions. They have responsibilities in common with respect to legislation, execution, and representation.

This chapter will explain that the working pattern for the group is a pyramid with the elevated presidency at the apex. That set of relationships applies to foreign as well as domestic relations. The last section, "Public Policy Interdependence," will explain that the group character of the House, the Senate, and the presidency depends upon mutual recognition of their common responsibilities in the realms of legislation, execution, and representation.

RESPONSIBILITIES OF THE ELEVATED PRESIDENCY

The component of the public policy superstructure that has changed most during the life of the U.S. constitutional system has been, of course, the presidency.[4] Analysts may differ on the extent of the change, depending on the degree to which they find subsequent developments to be implicit in the provision of the 1787 document. This book tends to attribute contemporary qualities to the later developments as well as to the original creations. Congressional authorization or approval has existed for many of the later changes so that there is a legitimate basis for the present-day presidency.[5]

The general trend of the development has been a movement from mere execution to administrative management and then still more to chief legislator and chief representative. It has been a series of elevations from administrative relations to congressional relations to public relations.[6]

Much of the elevation of the presidency has involved the use of public media in support of presidential aims and actions from the start to the finish of the political career.

The leading presidents of this century, Theodore Roosevelt, Woodrow Wilson, and Franklin Roosevelt, were masters in the use of public media. More recent presidents, particularly John Kennedy and Jimmy Carter, made new and greater use of television only to be outdone by Ronald Reagan. At times, there seems to be a media-minded government on top of the law-minded government.[7]

Contemporary presidents may be best known for their public, political personalities.[8] This high percentage absorption in media relations makes the constitutional system of today still more distant from the legislative Congress, the executive president, and the judicial court systems of the constitutional facade.

One scholarly analyst says what many assume, that is, "Today the president *is* the government for millions of Americans."[9] But that is not new. A hundred years ago, an analyst of government, struck by the public admiration of President Grant, wrote, "The tendency of all people is to elevate a single person to the position of ruler."[10] A quarter of a century ago, Clinton Rossiter put it this way: "The American people . . . have made the Presidency their peculiar instument."[11] Then in 1978 James MacGregor Burns's *Leadership* reminded us that the 1787 convention intended Congress and not the president to be the center of leadership and that the "alchemy of time" has transformed the presidency.[12]

It is not surprising, of course, that presidents deem themselves to be the government; many members of Congress and a good number of professors and journalists support this idea of the presidency, particularly in diplomatic and military affairs.[13]

The emphasis upon activism and public relations, to be found in such presidents as Andrew Jackson and Franklin Roosevelt, has become the hallmarks of political democracy. In 1898 Henry Jones Ford observed that as the presidential office has been constituted since Jackson's time, "American democracy has revived the oldest political institution of the race, the elective kingship."[14]

Chapter 1 noted that one of the forces of constitutional change is the belief of many U.S. citizens in "monocracy" or government by one. U.S. independence and national identity involved a protest against monarchy, and its citizens feel deeply that royalty is not for them, but they seem to revere the presidents as if they were kings. The key factors in that appeal may be unity and activity more than royalty or tradition. A relevant remark was made a century ago by the English historian Walter Bagehot concerning the unique intelligibility of the *monarchy*: "The mass of mankind understand it, and they hardly anywhere in the world understand any other." It is often said that men are ruled by their imagination, but Bagehot pointed out "it would be truer to say that they are governed by the weakness of their imaginations."[15]

Bagehot argued that the "nature of a constitution, the action of an assembly, the play of parties . . . are complex facts, difficult to know, and easy to mistake. In contrast, the action of a single will, the fiat of a single mind, are easy ideas; anybody can make them out, and no one can ever forget them."[16]

The leading contemporary analyst of presidential behavior asserts that "the President helps people make sense of politics."[17] In actual fact, many citizens assume that government is what the president does, or what he is. The president is a single personality, and even when he is only a figure of struggle, he can be understood, and ordinary people can relate to him.

The public relations presidency, discussed in Chapter 9, may appeal to many persons, but they are apt to be the "media public," that is, those attached to the drama and the contest of the popular media. Such persons seem less interested in the major political parties, and that may affect the public policy process. Two leading analysts present this conclusion:

> Over a relatively short period of time, a new sort of American political system is coming into being. Among its features are high degrees of mass participation in hitherto elite processes, the replacement of political parties with the news and publicity media as primary organizers of citizen action and legitimizers of public decisions, the rise in the influence of media-approved and media-sustained interest groups, and the decline of interest groups linked to party organizations.[18]

The efforts of presidents to surmount this media whirl are apt to draw them away from congressional relations. They are inclined to stress ideological positions rather than coordinative ones. The public relations presidency tends to be extended to the left or the right, according to ideological preferences, and thus is less able to guide the diverse factions of Congress in developing a unified legislative program. This book favors the elevation of the presidency to the position of public policy leader for the houses of Congress, which often requires a position that is near the center of the policy interests of Congress.

CONGRESSIONAL CONNECTIONS OF THE ELEVATED PRESIDENCY

The preceding section indicated that group achievement among the three elected institutions may require a near-center president. Is there a comparable challenge to the district and state representatives in the houses of Congress?

The simple answer is that all elected institutions have some common duties. Each is an integral part of the public policy superstructure. The ultimate duty of each is to help reconcile the policy conflicts among the citizenry and the government and especially among the elected institutions themselves. This is a higher function than either legislation or execution.

The more positive perception of Congress and the president involves recognition that they are not separate legislative and executive institutions but rather the representational group of the national government. There is need for transformation from origins in electoral politics to accomplishments in coordinative politics. [19]

The potentials for closer relationships among the three institutions will be considered. The most distinctive contrast is between the active unity of the presidency and the passive diversity of the houses of Congress. [20] This prompts a rather obvious question: Can there be mutual benefit from closer coordination? In other words, can the president gain from congressional diversity, and can Congress benefit from the impact of presidential unity?

Two 1985 books by leading political scientists deal with the contemporary problems of presidential-congressional relationships: *Constitutional Conflicts between Congress and the President* by Louis Fisher and *The Personal President: Power Invested, Promise Unfulfilled* by Theodore J. Lowi. Both conclude that presidents should be more subject to the legislated policies of Congress, but they differ on how these goals are to be achieved.

Fisher's book reviews pertinent developments in the Supreme Court, as well as in Congress and the presidency, since 1981 when he published a similar volume, *The Politics of Shared Power: Congress and the Executive.* [21] Both books present valuable analysis and appraisal of the constitutional status of relationships, and they conclude with strong demands for more legislative guidance or even control of the presidency. There are such statements as the following:

> To remain consistent with the Constitution, executive authority and administrative discretion should be directed and channeled by legislative policy [p. 326].
>
> We will never be able to define with any precision the meaning of executive and legislative, or show where one branch fades and begins to blend into the other. Still, the general theory and practice of separated powers can be retained [p. 326].

Congress must be willing to participate actively in questions of
national policy, challenging the President and contesting his actions.
It cannot be viewed as quarrelsome behavior for Congress to assess
presidential action independently. Issues need the thorough explora-
tion and ventilation that only Congress can provide [p. 334].

"With all its deficts, delays and inconveniences, men have discovered no technique for long preserving free government except
that the Executive be under the law, and that the law be made by
parliamentary deliberations" [p. 334].[22]

Fisher's book ends with the above quotation from the opinion of the
late Supreme Court Justice Robert Jackson in the steel seizure case
of 1952. In that decision, as noted in Chapter 11, the Court held that
President Truman, even during the Korean War, could not use a
procedure that Congress had not approved and may have rejected.

The suggestion is that we should not view Congress and the
president merely as separate legislative and executive powers. There
is much more to their high-level roles as the representational group
or branch of the national government. Their superstructure functions
place considerable priority on common responsibilities in both
governmental and representational areas.

The activist unity of the presidency and the passive diversity of
Congress cannot be brought into working relationship via the execu-
tive-legislative formula. The more positive perception is to conceive
of them as politically separated institutions sharing the functions of
representation and public policy making.

Lowi is equally disturbed by the unbridled presidents of the
Vietnam War period. He not only assumes that Congress should control the presidency by legislative means; he also suggests means,
sometimes elaborate ones, by which Congress can turn the presidency into "a more parliamentary office."[23] These include stronger
political parties, even a strong third party, and congressional selection of presidents, and possibly constitutional amendments that may
alter the presidential nominating process and, for the elected president, the method of selecting the cabinet.

The strongest attack is upon the "plebiscitary Presidency," that
is, the presidency guided or controlled only by the election and
occasional plebiscites on particular issues. This will be referred to
here as the Congress-free presidency. Lowi's concluding section tells
how to "build down" the presidency.

Here, again, there is little recognition that the problem is not only presidential selection but also the separate selection of the two houses of Congress. The three elections are sufficiently separate that the institutions are deeply separate politically. How can they best fit together in the making of a common public policy? This work has continually stressed the operating formula of the three-piece pyramid, connected at near center. This brings into operating relationship the active unity of the presidency and the grassroots diversity of the members of Congress. Yet coordination will not come without the will to accommodate and to agree upon adjustments.

ROLE OF CONGRESS WITH RESPECT TO THE MILITARY

The public and scholarly media may give the impression that the president as commander in chief has constitutional authority to act in military affairs independently of Congress.[24] Support for this belief is accentuated by an ever-present fear that quick action might be needed.

Chapters 4, 5, 7, 8, 10, and 11 have explained the constitutional authority of Congress with respect to military policy and the Supreme Court's general support of the congressional role. The real problem may be not whether Congress has the authority, but whether it has the will and the skill to use it. As previously noted, the first Congress enacted laws specifying the conditions under which President Washington could call out the militia.[25] Now the general tendency is for Congress to allow the president to act. The Supreme Court seems to require Congressional authorization of policy but at the same time appears anxious to accept indirect and delayed approval.

One decision of the Supreme Court that found prior authorization by Congress concerned the 1942 trial of Nazi saboteurs who entered the United States without their military insignia and thus were deemed to be violating the law of war.[26] They were tried before a military commission, although they had petitioned the Supreme Court for a civilian trial, asserting that a military trial had not been authorized. The Court denied the claim, and its explanation seems to be rather characteristic of its attitude.

The Court opinion first identified the constitutional authority of Congress and the president with respect to the defense of the nation. The Court pointed to seven enumerated powers (1, 10, 11,

12, 13, 14, and 18) providing Congress with power to act in defense matters. The Court identified four presidential authorizations: "executive power," the "take care" clause, the commander in chief provision, and the power to appoint officers. The Court then summarized:

> The Constitution thus invests the President as Commander in Chief with the power to wage war which Congress has declared, and to carry into effect all laws passed by Congress for the conduct of war and for the government and regulation of the Armed Forces, and all laws defining and punishing offenses against the law of nations, including those which pertain to the conduct of war. . . .
>
> It is unnecessary for present purposes to determine to what extent the President as Commander in Chief has constitutional power to create military commissions without the support of Congressional legislation. For here Congress has authorized trial of offenses against the law of war before such commissions.[27]

The invasion of the United States by the Nazi saboteurs was a unique and unexpected event, but the acts of Congress were sufficient in type and scope to permit the president to deal with the matter through procedures and practices authorized by Congress.

The foremost attempt of Congress in contemporary times to limit a "fast-acting" president in the use of military forces is the "War Powers Resolution of November 7, 1973" (Public Law 93-148; 87 Stat. 555).[28] This was a joint resolution adopted by a Congress disturbed by the actions of Presidents Johnson and Nixon in sending armed forces to Southeast Asia. The resolution was passed over the veto of President Nixon. It allows the president to introduce armed forces where hostilities exist or are imminent only pursuant to a declaration of war, specific statutory authorizations, or a "national emergency created by an attack upon the United States, its territories or possessions, or its armed forces."

Consultation is required "in every possible instance" before committing armed forces to a situation where hostilities exist or are imminent. Also, the president must report within 48 hours to the Speaker of the House, and the president pro tempore of the Senate, if armed forces are introduced where hostilities exist or are imminent, or if there are certain other specifically defined employments of the forces.

The clout of the resolution is probably in the provision that troops committed to a hostile situation are to be withdrawn after 60 days unless Congress has declared war or enacted a specific authorization or if Congress cannot meet because of an armed attack upon the United States.

Allowances of additional time are stated in detail. The president may have an added period of 30 days if he certifies to Congress that such time is needed for safe withdrawal of the armed forces. Also, forces engaged in hostilities outside the United States, without a declaration of war, or specific statutory authorization, are to be removed if Congress by a concurrent resolution so directs. According to the general rule, such a resolution would not be subject to presidential veto.

The element of the 1973 War Powers Resolution that presidents most criticize seems to be the provision that a commitment of forces must be terminated unless Congress takes a certain action within a specified period. Thus Congress may terminate the commitment simply by doing nothing. That, of course, may happen if Congress cannot agree on what to do. A president who wishes to keep troops in a foreign territory must convince Congress to take a certain action. This would seem to test the president less as commander in chief than as politician in chief.

Congressional-presidential relations under the War Powers Resolution may come within their general experience and that is hard to predict. Chapters 10 and 11 explained that often the constitutional limits of presidential authority may not be clear. Also, Congress has many times given presidents discretionary power to act in emergency situations. In addition, Chapter 11 explained that Congress at times has ratified or legitimated the actions of presidents taken without definite authority.

PUBLIC POLICY INTERDEPENDENCE

Many citizens may assume that Congress and the president have separate functions, but they actually have three common functions— legislation, execution, and representation. Moreover, in each area, the group is responsible for the higher levels of public policy.

The Supreme Court has disapproved presidential independence even in foreign affairs. Chapter 11 showed that the Court ruled against a president acting on his own in seizing steel mills during the

Korean War. There, Justice Jackson stated that the Constitution "contemplates that practice will integrate the dispersed powers into a workable government."[29]

The Court approved that statement in two subsequent cases. One involved President Nixon's refusal to surrender tape recordings wanted in a criminal trial, and the other upheld President Carter's agreement on financial matters with Iran during the hostage situation.[30] Moreover, in this last case, the Court found that Congress had approved the presidential practice of making special agreements in foreign affairs emergencies. Each Supreme Court action appears to provide precedent for considering the elected institutions as sharing common responsibilities.

These situations seem to apply Montesquieu's idea of action in concert among the three politically separated institutions of the "fundamental constitution"—the democratic and aristocratic branches of the legislature and the veto-empowered monarch.

From the start this book has stressed three points. First, the houses of Congress and the presidency make up a separate group. Second, they function as a public policy superstructure. Third, they are born politically separated, and they have common responsibilities, rather than separated functions like the other governmental units.

These elected institutions have the special policy duty of trying to integrate public interest conflicts. In such an endeavor there must be give and take. At the start there may be the politics of confrontation, but the goal is policy development and accommodation. To attain that end they must engage in a good deal of coordinative politics.

The interactions of the three institutions among themselves combine competition and coordination. The dependence of the president upon the two houses of Congress is emphasized in the following observations:

> Through the radio and the press the president may seek to maintain his national constituency; but in actual exercise of his power he must seek day-to-day assent of the particularism of political forces represented in Congress and in local machines. The president is commonly thought of as representing the general welfare; Congress is the tool of "special interests." In fact, presidential policy, however "pure" in motivation, must mean the promotion of certain interests at the expense of others.[31]

> The president must influence Congress because he generally cannot act without its consent.[32]

> The American Constitution requires both branches of the legislative body and the Chief Executive to come to an agreement not only on major questions of policy but also on major matters of administration.[33]

> In actuality, many of the President's foreign-affairs powers are shared with Congress, particularly the Senate.[34]

The last observation touches upon the most troublesome area because there is a fairly common tendency to believe that presidents are much less dependent in matters of foreign affairs and national security than in domestic matters. The Constitution, as shown in Chapter 5, places a good deal of discretion in Congress with respect to laws concerning military and foreign issues. But scholars as well as observers generally tend to make presidents special in this area. However, the difference is relative. Moreover, there is increasing difficulty in separating issues between foreign and domestic.

High policy interdependence includes not only presidential dependence upon Congress but also the reliance of the Senate and the House upon both the presidential and the executive systems. This is expressed by a scholarly analyst of Congress:

> In the administrative process the Executive leads; the Congress controls. In the legislative process the normal situation is no different. The legislature is not the dominant influence in the legislative process. The President is more influential. He leads and Congress controls. Leadership in this context means two things: to initiate the legislative process, that is, to perform its early stages, and to impel it, or to continuously drive the process forward.[35]

The increasing diversity of the organization of the houses makes the active unity of the presidency even more necessary. This has been recognized quite pointedly by commentators for a considerable period:

> Practice under the Constitution clearly demonstrates that the legislative process requires presidential guidance.[36]

Congress increasingly looks to the President to submit a legislative program and devotes most of its attention to his proposals.[37]

Today, the president has become the keystone of the legislative process. . . . No other public figure is capable of using his prestige to reconcile feuding factions and lead them boldly and consistently in a particular policy direction.[38]

In summation, we will present the following general comments upon the group character of the elected institutions. These institutions clearly exemplify a case where the whole is greater than the sum of the parts. Each of the three institutions is an official representative of the active voting citizenry of the United States. But each is definitely subordinate to the compound force of the three institutions. Each represents the nation in a different way. The House of Representatives acts through the combined majority force of the separately elected representatives of 435 districts. The Senate acts through the combined majority force of 100 senators chosen separately by the 50 states of the Union. The president is the choice of the majority of the 538 members of the 50 electoral colleges in the 50 states. Thus there are three separate channels of representation each with a different electoral message.

The determination of a composite electoral position from the three separate electoral positions would seem to be the most important aspect of the whole constitutional and political system of the national government. But it is also one of the most neglected aspects of the system. In fact, there is a much greater tendency to interrupt than to facilitate the determination of a composite program, which indicates a faulty pattern of interaction. The general tendency may be to impose functional separation upon voter separated institutions. Yet closer examination of their situation and the problems of government suggests the need for considering them to be a "mixed constitution" and with shared functions.

NOTES

1. Pendleton Herring, *Presidential Leadership* (New York: Farrar and Rinehart, 1940), p. 1.

2. Clinton Rossiter, *The American Presidency*, rev. ed. (New York: New American Library, 1962), p. 250.

3. Hugh Heclo, "Introduction: The Presidential Illusion," in Heclo and Lester M. Salamon, eds., *The Illusion of Presidential Government* (Boulder, Colo.: Westview Press, 1981), p. 2.

4. "The American presidency was not designed to be the center of leadership in the new republic. . . . The alchemy of time transformed the role of the President into what has more recently been called the imperial and even the omnipotent presidency." George MacGregor Burns, *Leadership* (New York: Harper & Row, 1978), p. 385.

5. See Chapter 11.

6. "The media perform four basic functions for presidents and other chief executives. . . . Fourth, the media allow the chief executives to remain almost continually in full public view on the political stage, keeping their human qualities and professional skills always on display." Doris Graber, *Mass Media and American Politics* (Washington, D.C.: Congressional Quarterly Press, 1980), pp. 194–95.

7. "Beginning with Kennedy the president became progressively less a man who presided over the processes of government in Washington and became progressively more a one man generator and executor of national policy." Joseph C. Harsch, "The Ford Presidency," *Christian Science Monitor,* March 6, 1975.

8. See, in general, Erwin C. Hargrove, *Presidential Leadership: Personality and Political Style* (New York: Macmillan, 1966).

9. William E. Mullen, *Presidential Power and Politics* (New York: St. Martin's Press, 1976), p. 1.

10. Henry C. Lockwood, *The Abolition of the Presidency* (New York: R. Worthington, 1884), p. 192.

11. Rossiter, *American Presidency,* pp. 251–52.

12. Burns, *Leadership,* p. 385.

13. See Chapter 11. "Presidential power certainly seems to be at its peak in foreign relations. . . . We must again emphasize, however, that there is inevitably a great deal of uncertainty in judgments about presidential power." Benjamin I. Page and Mark P. Petracca, *The American Presidency* (New York: McGraw-Hill, 1983), pp. 343, 376.

14. Henry Jones Ford, *Rise and Growth of American Politics* (New York: Macmillan, 1898), pp. 284, 293. See Robert S. Hirschfield, ed., *The Power of the Presidency,* 2d ed. (Chicago; Aldine, 1973), p. 251.

15. Walter Bagehot, *The English Constitution* (1867); reprint ed. (London: Oxford University Press, 1928), p. 30.

16. Ibid.

17. James David Barber, *The Presidential Character* (Englewood Cliffs, N.J.: Prentice-Hall, 1972), p. 5.

18. Nelson W. Polsby and Aaron Wildavsky, *Presidential Elections: Strategies of American Electoral Politics,* 5th ed. (New York: Charles Scribner's Sons, 1980), pp. 218–40, 272–86.

19. See the section entitled "The Concept of Coordinative Politics" in Chapter 9.

20. Louis W. Koenig, *The Chief Executive,* 4th ed. (New York: Harcourt Brace Jovanovich, 1981), p. 157.

21. Louis Fisher, *The Politics of Shared Power: Congress and the Executive* (Washington, D.C.: Congressional Quarterly Press, 1981), pp. 209–11.

22. Louis Fisher, *Constitutional Conflicts between Congress and the President* (Princeton: Princeton University Press, 1985), pp. 326, 334.

23. Theodore J. Lowi, *The Personal President: Power Invested and Promise Unfulfilled* (Ithaca, N.Y.: Cornell University Press, 1985). "The most constructive approach to building down the presidency would be the strengthening of political parties. If party organizations returned to the center of presidential selection, they would build down the presidency by making collective responsibility a natural outcome of the selection process rather than an alien intruder." Ibid., p. 209.

24. See, for instance, Robert Scigliano, "The War Powers Resolution and the War Powers," in Joseph M. Bessette and Jeffrey Tulis, eds., *The Presidency in the Constitutional Order* (Baton Rouge: Louisiana State University Press, 1981), pp. 115–53; Erwin C. Hargrove and Michael Nelson, *Presidents, Politics, and Policy* (Baltimore: Johns Hopkins University Press, 1984), pp. 20–24; 246–49.

25. See Chapter 7.

26. *Quirin, ex parte,* 317 U.S. 1 (1942); ibid., p. 26.

27. Ibid., p. 26.

28. *Public Law* 93–148; 87 U.S. *Statutes at Large* 55.

29. See the section entitled "Supreme Court Rejection of Presidential Independence" in Chapter 11.

30. *United States v. Nixon,* 418 U.S. 633, 703, 704 (1974).

31. Herring, *Presidential Leadership,* p. 9.

32. George C. Edwards III, *Presidential Influence in Congress* (San Francisco: W. H. Freeman, 1980), p. 35.

33. Leonard White, *The Federalists* (New York: Macmillan, 1947), p. 50.

34. Louis W. Koenig, *Congress and the President* (Chicago: Scott, Foreman, 1965), p. 68.

35. Arthur Maass, *Congress and the Common Good* (New York: Basic Books, 1983), p. 10.

36. Edward S. Corwin, *The President: Office and Powers, 1787-1948* (New York: New York University Press, 1948), p. 364.

37. Joseph P. Harris, *Congress and the Legislative Process,* 2d ed. (New York: McGraw-Hill, 1972), p. 127.

38. Frank Kessler, *The Dilemmas of Presidential Leadership: Of Caretakers and Kings* (Englewood Cliffs, N.J.: Prentice-Hall, 1982), p. 162.

CONCLUDING COMMENTS

We will begin these final remarks by considering the ten "fundamental questions" presented in Chapter 1:

1. The idea of integrated powers should be applied to the houses of Congress and the presidency because they are the elected institutions of the national government.

There have been several changes in the scope and quality of the election system. Three institutions are now chosen, in effect, by popular vote, and the threefold character of the electoral system results in each institution receiving a distinct message from the voters. The result is that the three are politically separated, and those differences override the separation of legal functions by which Congress and the president are identified in the first sentences of Articles I and II of the Constitution.

Thus the houses of Congress and the president, as the three elected institutions of the national government, are now in a special category. As noted in Chapter 12, they are burdened with multiple separations, including the common belief that Congress is simply the legislative branch and the president is simply the executive branch. At the same time the increased need for determining public policy and enacting legislation, and the more extensive disunity in the houses of Congress, mean that there is increased need for coordinated effort by the president and the houses of Congress.

The doctrine of separated powers is one type of checks and balances, designed to prevent undue concentration of power. Now, the political separations and other causes of disunity among the three elected institutions make inaction rather than concentration the major threat to freedom and welfare.

2. The elected institutions should be perceived as being a separate group. Both "representational group" and "public policy superstructure" are helpful designations. We need to perceive of them as having common functions of a high level.

3. There has been substantial fusion of legislative and executive powers, and both Congress and the president are responsible for both systems. Chapters 4, 5, and 6 explained the diversity of constitutional grants. The mixture and fusion increased with the adaptation of the constitutional system, as noted in Chapters 7, 8, and 9. The

Supreme Court has approved much delegation of rule-making authority by Congress to the president and the executive departments.

Chapter 5 found that the Constitution gives Congress substantial authority over foreign and military policies, although there may be difficulties in that arrangement. However, the Supreme Court has emphasized both the authority of Congress and its substantial application of that power.

4. The group of elected institutions is an example of separated institutions sharing functions. Congress and the president may appear in the facade of the Constitution to be separated by different legal functions, but now their deep involvement in the election and representation systems causes their basic separation to be institutional and political. At the same time, legislative and executive operations have become increasingly fused or mixed. Accordingly, they have common responsibilities with respect to legislation, execution, and representation.

5. The pattern of separate legislative, executive, and judicial functions is particularly relevant to the processes of criminal law. Chapter 13 noted that Montesquieu relates this arrangement to the political liberty of the subject or citizen, and he says that such liberty depends upon the "goodness of the criminal laws." The U.S. defense lawyer James Otis apparently was the first to quote Montesquieu, which was in protest to the English enforcement methods in the early stages of the independence movement.

6. The developmental roots of U.S. government include both the classical concept of the "mixed constitution" and the more modern pattern of legislative-executive-judicial separation. As explained in Chapter 2, the two ideas were apparent in the English constitutional system of 1700, and both were adopted or adapted by the American Founders.

7. This study asserts that basic differences existed at the Constitutional Convention between the "national executive" and the "President of the United States." That may be contrary to the common belief. As explained in Chapter 4, the "executive" was something between the legislative and the judiciary, while the president had a dozen roles of wide variety.

8. The Constitution gives Congress much authority over the executive system and assigns the president initiating roles with regard to the legislative process. See Chapters 4 and 5.

9. This study contends that the Constitution gives Congress much authority with respect to foreign as well as domestic policy. There are many opinions to the contrary. It must be recognized that Congress is slow-acting, while the president is fast-acting. Congress may need to authorize in anticipation, or it may need to consider action after the fact.

10. This study may be unusual in (1) recognizing that the "representational group" is, in effect, a legitimating agency for issues that the Supreme Court will not accept as juridical; (2) considering that "checks and balances" is a general principle of limitation and that there are three patterns of "separation of powers" in support of that principle; and (3) maintaining that the three elected institutions have a common obligation to determine, on the basis of the three electoral messages, a composite public policy for the guidance of the public and the government.

In conclusion, the primary aim of this book has been to explain a more constructive way of perceiving the relationships of the presidency, the Senate, and the House of Representatives, in their guidance and scrutiny of the legislative and executive systems and in their representation of the active citizenry of the nation.

This study has reviewed and analyzed the important structures of the national government and the developments during the 200 year life of the U.S. constitutional system as well as its present operations. From almost every angle, there is clear evidence that achievement is hampered by the multiple separations among the three elected institutions. Numerous analysts of Congress and the presidency call for cooperative efforts. Repeatedly, we see the need for the idea that these separated institutions have common functions and that they should approach their duties in the spirit of coordination.

Both the public and the elected officials might benefit from a more positive perception of this representational group. There is surely much need, on all sides, for a general willingness to act in relation to a composite public policy based upon the three electoral messages received by the houses of Congress and the presidency from the active voters of the United States. In terms of constitutional theory, that involves the concept of separated institutions sharing the public policy guidance of legislation, execution, and representation.

INDEX

Morris, Gouveneur, 41
Morris, Robert, 26, 91
Morrow, William, 120-21, 128
Mullen, William T., 124, 129
multiple separation pressures upon elected institutions, 3-6, 99-100, 104-07, 165-67, 171-74, 206-08. *See* congressional disunity; electoral disjunctions; political party conflicts; public interest conflicts

National infrastructure, 18-19, 28, 93-95, 187
national sovereignty, *see* division of national sovereignty
necessary and proper clause, 50-53, 63-64, 132-33
Neustadt, Richard E., 5, 124, 129
new perception of congressional/presidential interactions, 2-4, 7, 99-100, 143-44, 208
Nixon, President Richard, 126, 199
Nourse, Joseph, registrar of the treasury, 1781-1829, 27

Operational condition of appointed officials: legal and functional separation, 36-37, 40, 75-77, 187
operational condition of elected institutions, political and institutional separation, 99-100, 123, 125, 164, 166-67
operating objective of appointed officials: legal conformance to acts of Congress, 18-19, 93-98, 188-89
operating objective of elected institutions: political coordination, 113, 120-21, 164-65, 184-86, 201-04
Orfield, Gary, 110, 116
Orth, Charles P., 82, 85
Otis, James, 187

Page, Benjamin I., 72, 204
Patterson, Justice William, 35

Peltason, J. W., 83
Petracca, Mark P., 72, 204
Pfiffner, James P., 44, 64
Pinckney, Charles, 33, 52
Pious, Richard M., 186, 191
Plato: *Laws*, 15
political coordination, 118-21, 193-97, 200-04. *See* operational objective of elected institutions
political separation of elected institutions, 2, 80-82, 99-100, 113
politicalization of the state executives in 1776, 22
political parties, 99-100, 106-07
political party conflicts, 2, 7, 99-100, 173, 194-95
politics, source, 119; system, 119
Polsby, Nelson W., 167, 178, 195, 204
Polybius, 15
powers, *see* functional integration of elected institutions; institutional separation of Congress and presidency
presidency, executive, 36-40, 52-53, 75-77; more than executive, 54-55, 70, 73-74, 77-80. *See* elevated presidency
president of the United States, title replacement of "national executive," 54-55.
presidential allegiance to public political system, 120
presidential character, 122; personality, 81
presidential/congressional relationships: domestic policy, 132-35, 200-03; foreign policy, 135-40; military policy, 91-92, 144-54, 198-200
presidential dependence upon Congress, 52-53, 192, 196-97
presidential growth, 55, 70, 80-82; political leadership, 118-21, 127-29; shift from administrative to

ABOUT THE AUTHOR

Henry J. Merry is a Professor Emeritus of Political Science of Purdue University, living at Ann Arbor, Michigan. He has undergraduate and law degrees from the University of Michigan, and holds an M.A. in Political Science from American University, an LL.M. from Harvard University, and a Ph.D. from the London School of Economics and Political Science. Before joining the Purdue faculty, he was an associate professor at Northern Illinois University.

Previously, for several years, he engaged in legal work in private and public positions. His 12 years of service with the national government included two years as legal analyst with the Legislative Reference Service, Library of Congress (1958–60), and five years as Chairman of the Excess Profits Tax Council of the Bureau of Internal Revenue (1947–52).

The author began analyzing the constitutional principles of checks and balances and the separation of powers in 1959, when he prepared studies for the Legislative Reference Service, including a memorandum on the power of Congress to regulate the appellate jurisdiction of the Supreme Court. That led to an article in the November 1962 issue of the *Minnesota Law Review:* "Scope of the Supreme Court's Appellate Jurisdiction: Historical Basis." This gave special attention to the activities of James Wilson, the leading Pennsylvania delegate, at the Constitutional Convention.

While teaching political science, after 1960, the author undertook an intensive study of the constitutional theories of Baron de Montesquieu. This resulted in his 1970 book on Montesquieu. Further study of constitutional distribution led to the publication of two books on separations within the executive system of the U.S. government.

His previous books are *Montesquieu's System of Natural Government*, Purdue University Studies, 1970; *Constitutional Function of Presidential-Administrative Separation,* University Press of America, 1978; and *Five Branch Government: The Full Measure of Constitutional Checks and Balances,* University of Illinois Press, 1980. His articles have appeared in the *American Bar Journal,* the *Western Political Quarterly* and the *Minnesota Law Review.* The American Bar Association in 1954 made him recipient of its Ross Essay Award for an essay on the Investigating Power of Congress.